UNDER SCOTT'S COMMAND

UNDER SCOTT'S COMMAND

LASHLY'S ANTARCTIC DIARIES

edited by

A. R. ELLIS
Lieut.-Commander, R.N.

*With an Introduction by
Sir Vivian Fuchs*

LONDON
VICTOR GOLLANCZ LTD
1969

First published April 1969
Second impression April 1969

575 00236 0

PRINTED IN GREAT BRITAIN
BY EBENEZER BAYLIS AND SON, LTD.
THE TRINITY PRESS, WORCESTER, AND LONDON

CONTENTS

Page

Introduction   9

Part I   The Voyage of the *Discovery*

1   The *Discovery* and her crew   13
2   To the Antarctic   17
3   Learning the Hard Way   28
4   Winter Routine   36
5   A Weather Eye   43
6   First Sledge Trips   49
7   Preparing for Sea   59
8   The Western Journey   68
9   Freed from the Ice   85
10 Interlude   92

Part II   The Last Expedition

11 The Last Expedition   97
12 Preparations for the Southern Advance   103
13 Winter in the Hut at Cape Evans   108
14 Motor Party on the Polar Journey   116
15 Man-hauling   122
16 Last Supporting Party   136
17 The Search   149
18 Epilogue   157

LIST OF ILLUSTRATIONS

	Page
H.M.S. *Discovery* in her winter quarters	64
Ships at anchor in Robertson Bay	65
The *Terra Nova* in a gale	80
Chief Stoker William Lashly	81
Inflating meteorological balloons	81
Edge of the ice shelf	112
The Matterhorn Berg and Mt Erebus	113
His Master's Voice	128
Capt. Scott, Lieut. Bowers, Dr Simpson and P.O. Evans leaving on an early spring reconnaissance	129

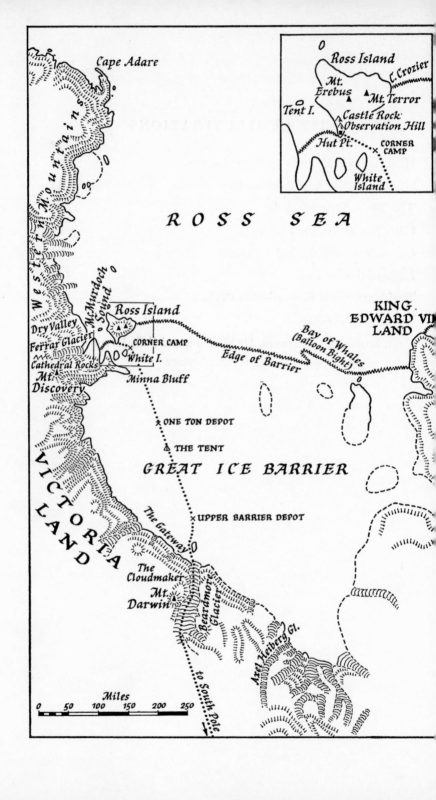

INTRODUCTION

by Sir Vivian Fuchs

THE STORY OF Captain Robert Falcon Scott's two expeditions is part of our national heritage. Through the years official accounts have been added to from the private records of his companions. In this book Chief Petty Officer Lashly's private diaries form the thread on which Commander Ellis has strung the events which culminated in the tragic loss of the polar party in 1912.

The author offers the story as a tribute to the naval ratings who took part in Scott's expeditions. Lashly himself emerges as an exceptional man, both in character and physical aptitude. But beyond this, it becomes clear how great was the interest of the lower deck in the scientific aims of the various journeys—the meteorological conditions, the collecting of specimens, the assessment and value of sledging rations and so on. Today this would not be surprising, but sixty years ago it was unusual. These ratings, by their self-imposed discipline and strength of character, bridged the wide gap which then normally existed between officers and men.

Perhaps one of the most striking things is that in spite of the laconic style of Lashly's writing one gains a sense of his imperturbability in the face of every situation. The dangers he himself incurred appear as minor episodes, embellished in this account only by quotations from Scott or other people; indeed Scott readily concedes that on one occasion he and Petty Officer Evans owed their lives to Lashly's cool courage.

One comes to realize that he represents the unselfish and dogged persistence which characterized all the ratings. They can hardly have had a very deep interest in scientific matters but they had a cause to which they dedicated themselves without reserve, and in doing so they earned the deep respect of their officers. As Scott wrote during the Western Journey, "I learn a great deal about lower deck life—more than I could hope to have done under ordinary conditions."

This book is a further contribution to our knowledge of the happy atmosphere which pervaded two polar expeditions. It was the combination of great leadership and loyal support which added an epic to our history.

PART I

THE VOYAGE OF THE *DISCOVERY*

List of Ship's Crew

Officers

Robert Falcon Scott	Captain, R.N.
Albert B. Armitage	Lieutenant, R.N.R.
Charles W. R. Royds	Lieutenant, R.N.
Michael Barne	Lieutenant, R.N.
Ernest H. Shackleton	Sub-Lieutenant, R.N.R.
George F. A. Mulock	Sub-Lieutenant, R.N.
Reginald W. Skelton	Lieutenant (E.), R.N.

Scientific Staff

Reginald Koettlitz	Surgeon and botanist
Edward A. Wilson	Surgeon, artist, vertebrate zoologist
Thomas V. Hodgson	Biologist
Hartley T. Ferrar	Geologist
Loius C. Bernacchi	Physicist

Men

David Allan	Petty Officer, R.N.
A. H. Blissett	Private, R.M.L.I.
Charles Clarke	Ship's Cook
Thomas Crean	Able Seaman, R.N.
Jacob Cross	Petty Officer, R.N.
George B. Croucher	Able Seaman, R.N.
Fred E. Dailey	Carpenter
James Dell	Able Seaman, R.N.
James H. Dellbridge	2nd Engineer
Edgar Evans	Petty Officer, R.N.
Thomas A. Feather	Boatswain
Charles R. Ford	Ship's Steward
Jesse Handsley	Able Seaman, R.N.
Clarence H. Hare	Able Seaman, R.N.
William L. Heald	Able Seaman, R.N.
Ernest E. Joyce	Able Seaman, R.N.
Thomas Kennar	Petty Officer, R.N.
William Lashly	Leading Stoker, R.N.
Arthur Pilbeam	Leading Seaman, R.N.
Frank Plumley	Stoker, R.N.
Arthur L. Quartley	Leading Stoker, R.N.

Gilbert Scott	Private, R.M.L.I.
William Smythe	Petty Officer, Vince R.N.
William J. Weller	Able Seaman, R.N.
Thomas Whitfield	Leading Stoker, R.N.
Frank Wild	Able Seaman, R.N.
Thomas S. Williamson	Able Seaman, R.N.

CHAPTER 1

THE *DISCOVERY* AND HER CREW

"THERE IS NOT one name on the list that does not recall to
me a pleasant memory or does not add to the splendid record
of loyalty and devotion with which I was served." Scott was
writing about his crew for the Voyage of the *Discovery*. He had
been serving as First Lieutenant of H.M.S. *Majestic* in the
Channel Squadron before joining the expedition, and he had
written to his friends in the other ships asking them each to
select one or two men from those who volunteered.

"It was a simple plan and relieved me of the difficulty of
picking out names from the very long list which would have
resulted had volunteers been generally called for. I knew well
that amongst British Bluejackets there would be no lack of good
men to volunteer for a voyage that promised to be so adventurous."

Scott had obtained a concession—"perhaps the most important which the expedition received"—to recruit from the
Navy. "From a very early date," he said, "I had set my mind
on obtaining a naval crew. I felt sure that their sense of
discipline would be an immense acquisition." The *Discovery* was
not in Government service so the ship and her company were
subject to the Merchant Shipping Laws, but as Scott explained:
"We lived exactly as though the ship and all on board had been
under the Naval Discipline Act; and as everyone must have been
aware that this pleasing state of affairs was a fiction, the men
deserve as much credit as the officers, if not more, for the fact
that it continued to be observed . . . For my part I can but say

that success in such an expedition as ours is not due to a single individual, but to the loyal co-operation of all its members, and therefore I must ever hold in grateful memory that small company of petty officers and men who worked so cheerfully and loyally for the general good.".

Lashly was one of the chosen volunteers. He was a Leading Stoker, aged 33, and had just re-engaged to serve for a further ten years to complete time for his pension. Born and brought up at Hambledon, he was one of a family of three boys and two girls. At 13, after attending the church school in the village, he had gone to work on the land with his father, who was a thatcher. One of his brothers became a thatcher, but life on the land was hard, and the family had to exist on what could be grown or raised locally. His other brother left home to be a soldier. Living as they did almost in the shadow of the great naval yard at Portsmouth, with men-of-war an everyday sight in Spithead and the Solent, it was not surprising that one of the family should want to go to sea. On 1st January, 1889, at the age of 21, William Lashly joined the Navy. After a short spell of service in the Persian Gulf and Indian Ocean, he was drafted to H.M.S. *Terror* in October, 1889, for three years' service on the West Indies Station. Back home again, he married in 1896, and his daughter was born four years later.

From the Warrant Officers' Mess, halfway across the great divide between officer and men of that time, C. R. Ford recorded his observations about the ship's company and Lashly in particular:

"The Naval personnel of the *Discovery* comprised as fine a body of men as could be found anywhere. The engine room staff were to some extent isolated as they worked a good deal in the engine room which in winter quarters was their work-shop. But I do know that Lashly was a man of fine character.

He was exceptionally reserved and even retiring in manner, always helpful to anyone needing help. I know that the Engineer, Skelton, thought the world of him."

Skelton knew Scott from *Majestic* days. Another old *Majestic* who joined the Expedition was Petty Officer Edgar Evans.

The men were well informed about the purpose of the voyage of the *Discovery*, and many of them had read up accounts of previous explorations.

"The objects of the expedition," said the sponsors' instructions to Scott, "are (a) to determine, as far as possible, the nature, condition, and extent of that portion of the South Polar lands which is included in the scope of your expedition; and (b) to make a magnetic survey in the southern regions to the South of the 40th parallel, and to carry on meteorological, oceanographic, geological, biological and physical investigations and researches. Neither of these objects is to be sacrificed to the other.

"We therefore impress upon you that the greatest importance is attached to the series of magnetic observations to be taken under your superintendence.

"It is desired that the extent of land should be ascertained by following the coastline; that the depth and nature of the icecap should be investigated, as well as the nature of the volcanic region, and of the mountain ranges, and specially of any fossiliferous rocks.

"The chief points of geographical interest are as follows: to explore the ice barrier of Sir James Ross to its Eastern extremity; to discover the land which was believed by Ross to flank the barrier to the eastward, or to ascertain that it does not exist, and generally to endeavour to solve the very important physical and geographical questions connected with this remarkable ice formation.

"If you should decide to winter in the ice your efforts as

regards geographical exploration should be directed to three objects, namely—an advance into the Western mountains, an advance to the South, and an exploration of the volcanic region."

CHAPTER 2

TO THE ANTARCTIC

LASHLY JOINED THE *Discovery* in London on 30th June, 1901, and the ship sailed for Spithead a month later. After two days at home in Hambledon he was back on board for the *Discovery* to anchor off Cowes, where she was inspected by the King and Queen, before sailing for Madeira on 7th August. Lashly started a diary on leaving London and kept it going for the next two and a half years. His private chronicle of the "Voyage of the *Discovery*" was written up in a stiff-backed ledger book, sometimes in pencil, but mostly in pen. Dates were often bracketed together when nothing unusual occurred but no item of interest was allowed to pass without being faithfully recorded.

After a run ashore at Funchal they coaled ship; "54 tons, washed down, and got under way." They were to call at South Trinidad before making for Cape Town, under sail when the wind was favourable, otherwise steaming. Lashly was not impressed by the ship's progress under sail.

17th/31st August. At sea steaming, ship won't sail fast enough to keep herself warm. Crossed equator at noon, stopped engines at 12.30 for repairs, a good breeze blowing. Father Neptune came on board and christened some of the officers and men that had not sailed in the Southern Seas before. A very good afternoon's sport.

On 1st September they were still under sail, "Making good

B 17

defects in the engine room of which we have plenty." They reached South Trinidad "which is situated in the South Atlantic off Brazil" on 13th September.

13.9.01 Sighted the island at day break. Captain, Engineer and Scientist landed. Could not drop anchor—too much water. Laid to all day, tried to catch fish, but no luck—too many sharks and too deep water.

There was no change of diet but "we get plenty of food and very good, but no bread—all biscuit". They left the island again at 6.30 that evening bound for the Cape "where we shall be overdue". It was an uneventful passage under steam and sail with one spell of "rather heavy weather—ship rolling a good deal, but very stiff—has proved herself a good sea boat." And later, "Wind dying away, shall be under way with steam before morning."

The Leading Stoker's forecast was correct. They arrived at Cape Town on 3rd October "nine days behind time", but he was very pleased to get his letters and books, and to hear that all was well at home. He was lying up with a bad knee on arrival but was up and about again by the time they got to Simonstown to store ship and refit at the Naval yard there. "Very nice little place Simonstown to look at—very high hills." He saw a Boer prisoners' camp and the ship was opened to visitors before sailing.

7.10.01 Bank holiday in Cape Colony. Hundreds of visitors—can hardly move for them, but they are all very nice. Governor of Cape Town, Sir Healy Hutchinson, came on board.

They sailed again on 14th October to begin the magnetic survey south of the 40th parallel of latitude, before making for

Lyttelton in New Zealand: "The ships in harbour gave us a splendid send off with all good wishes for a successful voyage, and a safe return to dear old England."

Lashly was always well informed about the ship's position: "Stopped for fishing on the Agulhas Bank. Caught several nice fish—some very good specimens." Then they were "Running the easting down—weather becoming colder with plenty of snow and rain. Very heavy sea running, ship rolling a good deal, but stands up well to it. Still on the same route, between 45 and 50 South latitude. Wind died out, under steam again. We are going south having passed 130° East longitude."

16.11.01 We are amongst the ice today—our first glimpse of what is to come later on. By 9 o'clock Saturday night we were blocked in the pack ice, can't move, raised steam to get out. We are now in 62° 50′ South 138° East this being somewhere due north of the south magnetic pole. We should go further south only time and coal will not permit. So we are going north calling at Macquarie Island on our way.

21.11.01 Called at Macquarie Island. Caught seals, penguins, hares, rabbits and numerous other things, also a lot of birds. Only stayed a few hours before we got under way again.

After experiencing "very heavy weather coming past Auckland—the ship rolled tremendously, but stood up well to it", they arrived at Lyttelton, the port of Christchurch, on 29th November, 1901: "When we got alongside there were hundreds to greet the *Discovery* and her crew."

Final preparations for the voyage south were made at Lyttelton and before they sailed "Bishop Julius held a special service on board, everybody attending." After sailing on 21st December Lashly wrote, "Our stay in Lyttelton has been a busy but pleasant one. I think the people are very nice in every thing and every way. They really seem to think we want a little enjoyment before we leave here. We had a splendid send off—all the ships in harbour came out to the heads and wished us God speed and safe return, but I regret to say that before we were clear of the ships one man, by name Bonner, fell from aloft and was killed instantly."

The *Discovery*'s crew were manning the yards to wave their farewells and Bonner, a young seaman, had climbed to the mainmast truck. He lost his balance when the ship met the first swell and fell to the deck still clutching the weather vane.

They were to call at Port Chalmers, the port of Dunedin, for coal.

23.12.01 Arrived at Port Chalmers. Funeral of Bonner and leave, I went up to Dunedin for a run. Came back 10.20 train and came on board.

Bonner was replaced by Able Seaman Thomas Crean who was lent from one of the ships of the New Zealand squadron, H.M.S. *Ringarooma*. Lashly did not remark on Crean's arrival, but this accident brought together the two men whose names were later to be linked in one of the greatest Antarctic stories. It would be difficult to imagine two more different types. Lashly was a man of very few words who went about his work humming quietly to himself with a contented smile on his face. Crean described himself as the "wild man from Borneo". He came from County Kerry and, like Lashly, was a strong, healthy, utterly dependable sort of man with a great zest for life.

24.12.01 Took in 25 tons of coal and ready to leave. A good send off from this place as we have from all others. A telegram was sent to London to bid farewell to those we have left behind us.

On Christmas day "we had service, but did not keep it up, we are going to keep it up when we get in the ice." On New Year's day 1902 they crossed the Antarctic circle. "We have been lucky and have only just come upon icebergs in latitude 66° South. There seems to be a channel away ahead of us—we are coming up to the pack ice now." Then they were in the thick of it. "It is a grand sight—caught some seals." And the next day, "it was seal liver for breakfast and seal steak for dinner. It is very good—better than beef, especially Bombay beef." The promised Christmas festivities passed with the laconic comment, "Xmas up". Lashly was busy lighting up another boiler. "The ice seems to be getting thicker than ever, we are going to try to push our way through but of course there is no telling how far it extends. We are far enough south not to have any night now. The first clear night the sun will be shining all night."

One day was spent taking in ice to be melted down with steam hoses for boiler water. Then, on 9th January, 1902, they were through the pack ice and into the open sea beyond. It had been a quick passage.

They reached Cape Adare at 7 p.m. on 9th January and the inquiring Lashly made a long entry in his diary. "Last night being clear the sun was shining beautifully all night—quite summer weather we are having now. Sighted Mount Sabine at 11.30 p.m. 120 miles off at the back of Cape Adare. I have been on shore for a look round. There is nothing here except volcanic eruption and stones. This is where the members of the *Southern Cross* wintered while they were here. The hut is still standing, some of the provisions are spoilt but others are in good condition and we shall leave them. There is also 15 tons of coal which we shall leave. I have also left a letter here to my wife—she may get it some day if the postman should happen to come this way. We are not staying long. The penguins here are of a much smaller kind, but they are plentiful enough. The ground and water is full of them—thousands of them. They are such funny birds like a lot of old men waddling along. We have caught three kinds of seal up to now, the crab-eater, the sea-leopard, and the Ross seal."

The *Discovery* cruised down the West coast of the Ross Sea looking for likely landing places and winter quarters. Lashly kept a watchful eye on proceedings:

11.1.02 Ice too closely packed. Can't get at Possession Island, we shall try and make Coulman Island.

12.1.02 Arrived off Coulman Island. The wind is freshening and we are expecting a gale. The land is very high so we are making for the lee of the land until the storm blows over. The wind is gradually increasing in force, we are steaming full speed in to it.

13.1.02 Storm still raging.

14.1.02 Storm cleared during forenoon. Posted records on Coulman Island on our way to Lady Newnes Bay. Plenty of seals here, taking in a winter stock of about 50. The ice is covered with them. We are working all night tonight.

15.1.02 The weather is settled now again. We are going on to Wood Bay to see if we can winter there. We captured the fourth kind of seal in Lady Newnes Bay—the Weddell seal. There are only four kinds known about here, none of them are fur seals, only hair seals.

18.1.02 Wood Bay frozen over still. Cannot get in. Mount Melbourne in the background.

19.1.02 Went into a bay this evening not yet named. Will make very good winter quarters. Found plenty of granite and also some moss growing.

20.1.02 Trying to find an opening between Mount Erebus and

Mount Terror. The pack ice is very close There is a big bay—McMurdo Bay—but no opening—land is in sight all round.

This was an optical illusion that had also deceived Ross. From where his ships were, at the seaward limit of the pack ice, Minna Bluff, the islands and Hut Point Peninsula gave the impression of continuous land round to Cape Crozier. Ross called it McMurdo Bay, but it is now called McMurdo Sound.

22.1.02 On our way to the barrier. Stopped at Cape Crozier and left official letters and private letters. I wonder if ever they will reach home. Very heavy swell, boat nearly capsized and drenched the crew, not very pleasant in this climate. Plenty of penguins here. We have come to the end of the land, now commences the great ice barrier. It is about 100 ft. high here and extends away to the south-east as far as the eye can see. It is still rising the further we go. We shall take a chain of soundings all along the barrier. The weather is all that can be desired very little below freezing, fine but cloudy.

24.1.02 Temperature is a good bit lower today. Lat. 78° 30 South, Long. 176° 00′ East. Still steaming along the barrier· Result of soundings from 300 to 400 fathoms. Mud at bottom.

25.1.02 Warmer along the barrier today. Plenty of very curious shaped icebergs. Sounding 312 fathoms, bottom mud. What an endless piece of ice.

26.1.02 Entered large bay in hope of finding opening through, but had to return as it was only part of the ice broken away. We are farther south today than any ship has ever been. Sounding 304 fathoms, mud. Stopped for dredging.

The curious shaped bergs were the flat tabular bergs of the Antarctic caused by large masses of ice breaking off from the floating seaward edge of the barrier which varied in height from a few feet to 250 feet above sea level. The barrier fills the southern half of the Ross Sea, like a flat shelf of ice, hinged to the coastline. Fed by the ice-cap slipping off the high continental plateau, its surface is a gently undulating plain of snow-covered ice, except where it comes in contact with the land or an island. These obstructions in the path of its slow glacier-like progress to the sea cause the barrier surface to be thrown up in confused pressure areas of high ice blocks and crevasses. The same occurs where the glaciers, coming down the mountains of the coastline, meet the barrier ice.

30.1.02 Heavy snowstorm, very cold. Plenty of pack ice and signs of heavy pressure. Land in sight. So we have passed the ice-barrier at last. Soundings 90 and 130 fathoms. Dredging very good.

This was the land that Ross had believed lay to the east of the barrier. It was christened King Edward VII land.

31.1.02 Very fine glaciers coming from the mountains. Tied up to iceberg and watered ship. Found some very fine specimens of Emperor Penguins.

The next day was an anxious one.

1.2.02 We are in the same place as yesterday. There seems a chance of having to stay here as the ice is rapidly forming up round us. We have been steaming round and round to try and get out, and at last we found the opening. Now for getting back to try and secure quarters for the winter.

Before that though, there was one more job to be done, and the ship was secured alongside the barrier in a little bay which was christened Balloon Bight, and later called the Bay of Whales. Although Scott did not realize it at the time this bay was a permanent feature of the barrier.

Sir Joseph Hooker, a survivor of the Ross expedition, had suggested ballooning to Scott. The War Office had supplied two balloons for the purpose and balloon section, of which Lashly was a member, had been sent to Aldershot for instruction. Scott wrote: "Although officers and men had regarded their short course as a most excellent diversion, they had picked up most of the wrinkles and had learnt to proceed about their work in the most businesslike manner."

Lashly took up the tale:

3.2.02 Weather fine and clear. Ran into bay and landed on the barrier. Sledge party leaving ship to go south to take observations. Balloon party got up gear ready for an ascent tomorrow if fine enough.

4.2.02 Weather fine but a little too much wind at first for ballooning. It died away at 8 o'clock and we prepared the balloon for inflating. It was rather a cold job. The skins being new had a great tendency to stick. However, we got through it very well, and in pretty good time after tearing the balloon twice and mending the same. Captain Scott made his first ascent up to about 700 feet. Afterwards Mr Shackleton and Mr Skelton went up and saw the sledge party about 20 miles away to the south. Could not keep the balloon inflated. The wind sprang up during the dinner hour and almost cleared the lot, but we managed to get it in with a damaged valve and one rent in the bottom part.

The balloon normally needed 16 cylinders, each containing

500 cubic feet of hydrogen, to inflate it properly. The temperature this day was 16° F. and a further three cylinders were needed before its name EVA could be read on its smooth taut side. Scott, who knew nothing of ballooning, went gaily up to 500 feet. Then he heard a cry of "sand" from below and remembered the bags at his feet. Instead of emptying them out gradually he began to sling them overboard wholesale. Eva, swaying perilously from side to side, shot up to 800 feet where it was checked by its mooring wire. When he got his breath back Scott was able to survey the empty barrier surface through his binoculars. There was nothing in sight. The mountains guarding the southern plateau and the Pole lay 400 miles to the south.

The rising wind caused Lashly and the other members of the balloon section to miss their turns at going up. It was probably just as well. Dr Wilson thought it was an "exceedingly dangerous amusement, and the training wholly inadequate". He went on, "If some of these experts don't come to grief over it out here, it will only be because God has pity on the foolish. Had any one used the valve in the morning it would not have closed properly and nothing could have prevented the whole show from dropping to earth like a stone." There is no mention of any more balloon ascents during the expedition.

7.2.02 Raised steam again. Got rather too close to the barrier to be pleasant. We have passed Cape Crozier, making for McMurdo Bay again. Very cold and heavy snowstorms.

The close shave he referred to occurred when the ship was in danger of being crushed between the barrier face and an iceberg.

8.2.02 We are going into McMurdo Bay round Mount Erebus

and Mount Terror and find they are, or what seems to be, an island. Landed party on the main land, or what seemed to be the main land. Did a little dredging with very good results.

9.2.02 Watered ship and church. This will be our winter quarters, here somewhere. Arrival Bay.

The mainland was the peninsula at the south-western corner of Ross Island which came to be known as the Hut Point Peninsula. The ship was to be frozen in, in the bay, where she would be protected from pressure, and the hut could be built nearby on shore.

10.2.02 Filling up with water again today. This looks like a dreary place to spend twelve months in, but we are going to set about it and make it as comfortable as possible. There are three huts to build, and the windmill to put up. Played football today on the ice. Very good game.

CHAPTER 3

LEARNING THE HARD WAY

THE WORK OF putting their home in order started straight away. One of Lashly's jobs was to rig the windmill which was to drive the dynamo for electric lighting. He spent long cold hours on it but was never enthusiastic about its prospects: "Windmill running fairly well, but wind varies too much. I don't think it will be of any great success." And, indeed, success was short lived. A month later: "Very heavy gale and snow storm blew the fans off the windmill. Another tiresome cold job. It is not nice handling iron with temperatures 10° or 20° below zero. We are going to repair the mill again, but I really don't think it will be of any use as the wind is so strong and boisterous." A fortnight later he was still "carrying on with the mill. We have to work when the wind don't blow, so we worked all day Sunday. Fancy! Up top of the old mill with the temperature 30° below zero. But we finished the top part about 8 o'clock Sunday night, and a good job too." Less than a week afterwards it was: "Very heavy gale blowing all day, and after our trying to get the windmill in working order it has totally collapsed this time." This was the last word on it, and the acetylene plant was brought into use for the rest of their stay.

Relaxations at this time included football matches on the ice: "Football match, officers versus men, resulted in a win for the officers two goals to one." But all through February and the first half of March the ice in the bay kept breaking up. The ship's moorings had to be shifted frequently, and Lashly sounded an indignant note: "The ice is breaking up all round us and away up the bay, or strait, for miles, completely spoiling our football ground."

17.2.02 Mr Ford away in evening skiing fell over a precipice and broke his leg in two places about 2½ miles from the ship. Sent out relief party and fetched him home in rather a frozen state.

19.2.02 A small sledge party consisting of Dr Wilson, Mr Ferrar and Lieutenant Shackleton to explore an island about 20 miles farther on.

The dog teams provided another diversion, amusing at the time, but with more serious implications. Their knowledge of the management and driving of dogs was non-existent: "Mr Armitage and Mr Bernacchi fitting out two teams of dogs ready for work." In fact, this was a trial race to discover whether stern measures or kindness produced the best results. To the accompaniment of wild cheering from the spectators Bernacchi's team won easily. Armitage, the advocate of force, never got started at all. As a result of this, when dogs were used for sledge journeys on this expedition, the men generally lent a hand on the traces. The dogs became even more reluctant to pull their weight and were never a success.

Besides being a liability on the sledges, the dogs fought amongst themselves: "The dogs are taking to killing one another, we lost two when they started fighting. The lot get on to one and settle him off. One of the best dogs got lost when away with the sledges, so that leaves us with twenty." And a little later: "We had another dog killed this morning. One of the best for pulling too. I hope we don't lose many more as they will be useful when we start sledging next spring." One brighter note: "Almost lost Joe Bernacchi, another dog today, he fell down a crevice, but managed to get him out." But again:

"Had another dog die today—this is running away with them and we shall want them badly later on when we begin sledging. But we have got an increase of four pups the other day. They are all doing well, poor little things, it is rather cold for them." Another time there were "seven more pups born last night— this makes fifteen, but one is dead. It is a wonder that the poor little things live in this climate." Two dogs were lost for three weeks, being found by two men out for a walk: "They had killed a seal and were living on it. One of them, having a chain on, got pinned under the seal and was half dead, the other that was free watched over him."

22.2.02 Wind too cold to work outdoors after breakfast. In evening had short lecture on frostbite and the best way to cure them if we do get them, which, now the weather is getting cold, we shall all be getting. Sledge party returned at 11 p.m.

By the end of February preparations for the first big sledge party were in full swing. Lashly did not go on this trip because he was still busy putting the base in order. Besides the wind-mill, there was the hut to be built ashore and provisioned against emergencies. There was no intention of living in it on this expedition, but it served as a vital staging post on sub-sequent expeditions. They stored it now with "eight months provisions, oil, and fifteen tons of coal". It was a useful addition to the amenities and provided storage space and a recreation room.

The sledge party was to go to Cape Crozier to post records of the *Discovery*'s whereabouts for future relief ships. A mail tin nailed to a post had been left there in the middle of a penguin rookery on the ship's earlier visit to Cape Crozier, but this had not contained exact details of winter quarters, which were not then known. Scott himself had intended to lead this party, but he had to withdraw at the last moment when he strained his knee while out skiing on slopes that had become rough and frozen hard. Lashly watched the preparations with interest and reported that: "They will, if successful, be away fourteen or fifteen days." In the light of experience Scott wrote of this party: "I am bound to confess that the sledges when packed presented an appearance of which we should afterwards have been wholly ashamed, and much the same might be said of the clothing worn by the sledgers. But at this time our ignorance was deplorable, we did not know how much or what proportions would be required as regards the food, how to use our cookers, how to put up our tents, or even how to put on our clothes. Not a single article of the outfit had been tested, and amid the general ignorance that prevailed the lack of system was painfully apparent in everything." Lieutenant Royds took over the leadership of the party having suffered no ill effects from falling overboard ten days before: "Being a good swimmer he got to the boat lying astern and came on board, not a very pleasant bath," said Lashly.

After seeing the sledge party off on 4th March, work on board went on quietly: "I was talking to Mr Ferrar who said, while they were out exploring, they came across some crystals which proved, when tested, to be epsom salts. So there is, or have been, a geyser about here at some period—a hot spring."

10.3.02 Sledge party seen returning in the distance. Waiting for news of what has happened.

This was the first bitter lesson in sledging and survival techniques in the Antarctic. Lashly went into some detail and made a long entry. Whether, if he had been in the party, his level-headed approach would have prevailed can only be speculation. Able Seaman Wild, who was in the party, later became one of the most intrepid explorers.

11.3.02 Well, this has been a very unfortunate day for us. Heavy snowstorm and tremendous wind—can't see a foot before you hardly. Temperature about 15° below zero. We are thinking of the sledge party all day and saying they ought not to come on in this weather, as it is almost fatal to get abroad in wind like this. We know they are getting close to the ship, but if they get into the tent and keep out of the wind they will be all right and won't get too many frost bites. But it appears that they struck camp this morning at 8 o'clock and proceeded on their way towards the ship. Arrived on top of the hill they pitched and had some lunch. The wind and snow increased. Some of the men got frost-bitten. Then thinking that they were not very far from the ship they struck tents and set out leaving sledges and all behind. This is a very dangerous place to start on such a day. They had not proceeded far before they lost Hare, he having gone back for his ski-boots. The whole lot turned tail to try and find him. While thus engaged Evans slipped on a glacier or slope and disappeared. Lieutenant Barne sits down and goes after him, the others waiting a time. Then Quartley goes and tries to find them, but did not return. So the others proceeded on their way to the ship. But they had not gone far before they all—Wild, Plumley, Heald, Weller, and Vince—went down an ice slope. Vince having fur boots could not bring up at all on the ice so went clean over the cliff into the sea below, and no way whatever of getting back. The others were utterly helpless. The snow was blinding and they could not see anything ahead of them. The only thing they could do was to try to get back to the top of the slope which they did under great difficulty. There were now five gone out of nine, leaving four. After roving about for some hours they finally reached the ship about 8.30 p.m. with the sad news of what had happened. A search party was at once prepared and a party sent round the coast to look along the shore in case of any of them being cast on an ice flow or anything. In the meantime we lit up one boiler and got steam so that we could draw their attention to the ship's whereabouts with the siren and Mr Armitage left the ship with the search party. Mr Barne, Quartley and Evans brought up on a slope and lost their bearings, and luckily just missed going into the sea. The siren gave them some clue to where they were, and they made tracks for the ship. The search party met them and found Mr Barne and Evans rather badly frost bitten. Quartley not quite so bad, but all three in more or less a dazed condition. Mr Ferrar accompanied them back to the ship. This was three more safe, leaving two still adrift. The search party went on to try and find Hare, but with no success whatever, returning to the ship at 3 a.m.

One reason the party had struck camp on the heights above the ship was that they could not get a hot lunch. The prickers of the primus stoves were broken. The whole party was somewhat demoralized and Vince and Hare had not even paused to put on their ski-boots before starting for the ship.

12.3.02 The wind still blowing. Today another search party sent out to look for Hare, but no result. It appears that Mr Royds, Skelton and Dr Koettlitz are going on to Cape Crozier with the despatches. The snow being too deep for anyone on foot to travel they have gone on ski taking enough provisions for fourteen days or reduced twenty-one days. We are all hoping they are safe."

13.3.02 Everything on as usual. Wind abated a good deal.

Everybody a bit down over the loss we have sustained, but just before dinner a pleasant surprise awaited us. While a party was working ashore someone was observed coming over the hill. Everybody was up to see who it was, as we never once doubted but that he was dead, if not gone into the sea, frozen to death as he had been 48 hours lost. It turned out to be young Hare and not frost-bitten at all. Of course there were some doubts about him, but poor old Vince was seen to go over into the sea where escape was impossible. It appears that Hare was roaming about for some time, must have fallen down and got buried in the snow, and went to sleep for 40 hours. When he awoke he found the sun shining on him. It was a marvellous escape from death, the temperature being about 30° below zero.

By 17th March, the ship was frozen in for the winter. There was one more sledge journey to be made to lay a depot of food in advance of next season's southern journey. Scott was to lead this party, but Lashly was still busy on board making all snug for the winter.

18.3.02 Another sledge party preparing to leave the ship to lay depot for party going south next year. Everybody seems to keep in good health. It is very healthy here, the air is absolutely pure. We live very well, sleep well and have plenty of work to keep ourselves employed and exercised. The days are getting short—we shall soon lose the sun for four months. It will be rather lonely and dreary during the winter.

22.3.02 Sledge party preparing to leave, but I am thinking the weather will cause a bit of trouble as the days are getting very short and much colder. The temperature is frequently below zero. Mr Skelton, Royds and Dr Koettlitz returned from sledging trip looking none the worse for their 17 days hard work, but it was impossible for them to reach Cape Crozier with despatches so we shall have another try next year. They were very much put out on hearing the accident to the others.

28.3.02 Good Friday. Sunday routine, also had hot cross buns or bricks, could not tell hardly which.

29th and 30th. Easter Holidays.

Lashly's gloomy prediction was correct. After only three days out: "The sledge party returned tonight after experiencing very rough weather and low temperatures. They were all more or less frost bitten. The temperature was as low as 60° below zero. No one can stand this sleeping out." This was the end of the first autumn's sledging and Scott's despondent report summed up the achievements to date: "In one way or another each journey had been a failure, we had nothing to show for our labours. The errors were potent; food, clothing, everything was wrong, the whole system was bad. It was clear there would have to be a thorough reorganization before the spring. That we were eventually able to make long and successful sledge journeys is no doubt due to the mistakes which we made and to the experience which we gained during the first barren attempts of this autumn, and yet more to the fact that we resolved to profit by them, and thoroughly take our lesson to heart."

CHAPTER 4

WINTER ROUTINE

AT THE BEGINNING of April they were stocking the larder for the winter.

7.4.02 Party over to Seal Bay killing and fetching seal meat on board. We get seal meat every other day. It is very good and I think is approved of by most on board.

8.4.02 Gale increased greatly today, but died away towards evening. A lot of Emperor Penguins came this way making tracks north. We collared 35 of them.

9.4.02 Photographed and weighed penguins today, the heaviest being 90 lbs. the largest on record.

10.4.02 Fine and nice. Party fetching more seal on board today.

A large seal lasted the ship's company two days. The liver was the favourite delicacy, but seals were never killed for the liver only. The whole beast had to be finished before the next was started. Dinner on Sundays was frozen New Zealand mutton: "Quite a treat to all hands," said Lashly, "but a few fresh vegetables would be acceptable." The vegetables were all tinned or dried. The interest in penguins went further than the pot, but penguin breasts made a good dish. Food was the same for officers and men and the men had their main meal at mid-day, followed by the traditional tot of Navy rum. Lashly was a lifelong teetotaller and never drank his tot. He appeared on the mess list as "Grog" so he drew his rum ration but always passed it on to his messmates. Strictly speaking this was illegal but it was a rule more honoured in the breach than the observance. He was a non-smoker too. "There are few non-smokers and no one who dislikes the smell of tobacco," wrote Scott referring to the rule that smoking was allowed on board at all times which was not normal Navy practice.

There was an ample issue of Navy tobacco supplied in leaf. The men rolled it into "pricks" with spun-yarn in the traditional way, and the atmosphere on the messdeck was generally pretty thick. One day "young" Hare was struggling with a pipe that would not draw so Lashly made him a three-pronged pipe-cleaner which Hare uses to this day. Lashly never commented on smoking or drinking.

The health of all hands was under the constant supervision of Dr Koettlitz and Dr Wilson. Regular monthly medical examinations were made which caused Scott to write: "One had but to cast one's eye over the records from the messdeck to realize what a splendid set of men we had from the point of view of physique." A specially strong instrument had to be used for measuring the grips of the men: "To prevent all chance of the ordinary one being wrecked." Lashly mentioned the inspections as they occurred, adding an occasional comment: "Still a slight increase in my weight. Health continues good. Hope it will continue the same always." Another time he said: "Result of blood first class condition. Weight still about the same, 176 lbs, measurements very satisfactory. Health of all hands very good up to the present."

Scott went to some lengths to describe the outstanding physique of Lashly and Petty Officer Evans. "Lashly, in appearance, was the most deceptive man I have ever seen. He was not above the ordinary height, nor did he look more than ordinarily broad, and yet he weighed 190 lbs and had one of the largest chest measurements in the ship. He was never in anything but the hardest condition." Of Petty Officer Evans he said: "A man of Herculean strength, very long in the arm and with splendidly developed muscles. He had been a gymnastic instructor in the Navy and had always been an easy winner in all our sports involving tests of strength. He weighed 178 lbs in hard condition."

Apart from the messdeck stove, Lashly had no complaints about living conditions: "The ship is fairly comfortable, there is nothing whatever to grumble about as we live well, sleep warm and nice, and have plenty of exercise. The only thing is we are troubled with a smoky stove when the wind is blowing hard. But I think other expeditions have always suffered with the same complaint." He never got to the root of this trouble and when the wind was in the South the stove smoked so much that they had to do without it: "Not nice with 52° of frost."

Weather permitting, all hands were expected to take half an hour's exercise out of doors each day, but no one was allowed to leave the ship alone: "Dr Koettlitz took our blood to examine it to see if we get enough exercise to keep us healthy." On one occasion: "We had another scare last night, three men asked permission to go for a short walk and were away from the ship five hours. Luck favoured them and the wind kept off, but it is so foolish to do such things as you cannot trust the weather five minutes." This incident happened only a few days after: "We were put in rather a stew again today, the boatswain and second engineer went for a walk and foolishly went too far. In the meantime it came on to blow which means almost for certain you are lost, but they turned up at the last moment. Three search parties were ready, but it was lucky they had not left the ship as it turned out a fearful night." Lashly had no patience with this sort of thing. He had already remarked after one blizzard that it was, "very dangerous to leave the ship alone as it is possible to get lost within 20 yards of her." His native respect for the weather stood him in good stead and he never got into difficulties through carelessness.

The ship's routine in the winter followed naval custom with practical adjustments to meet the unusual conditions. The Engine Room department were kept busy with a variety of jobs under the supervision of Lieutenant Skelton, "our invaluable engineer," as Scott called him. "The amount of mechanical work that is needed to make good every defect in such an expedition as this is truly surprising," Scott wrote in his report, "and the work varies from the roughest to the most delicate task. Without mechanical skill we should have been hopelessly at sea, and it is not too much to say that the majority of our scientific observations would have been brought to a standstill." Towards the end of May Lashly noted that: "We are still busy making and repairing things. Every day brings along some fresh job." Amongst other things he turned his attention to the ski boots: "In some cases they have been fitted with a stout sole by the cobbling abilities of that excellent man of all trades, Lashly," was Scott's comment. But on clothing in general Scott said: "I regret to say that the clothing issue displays the fact that the sailors are extremely careless of their clothes—of course there are the few careful ones by whom the others can be judged." In all the photographs Lashly always looked trim and neat. He was always clean shaven when on board which was not always the case with everyone else. He wore a little cross on a chain around his neck at all times. One of his messmates recalled that "he was always friendly and clean, both in his living and speech—in the latter respect outstandingly so for a lower deck rating."

Work in the winter normally went on till 1 p.m. dinner. Then, if there were no important jobs on hand, the men were free to do as they pleased. Scott set his face against making unnecessary work just to keep the men busy. The system worked well and they were never bored. Man-of-war routine was observed on Sundays with traditional mess deck rounds and the church service. "Usual amount of church today being Sunday." Lashly often remarked that the week seemed to pass pretty quickly.

The lighter side of life was well catered for with the *South Polar Times*, lectures, magic lantern shows and amateur theatricals. Shackleton was the editor of the *South Polar Times* which was a monthly paper and made its first appearance on 24th April. It was greeted by Lashly with the remark: "Of course it causes a little amusement." He became more enthusiastic with later issues: "The paper is a very good one, quite amusing and interesting, the illustrations are also good." The illustrations were mostly the work of Dr Wilson, but all contributions were anonymous. Another paper called the *Blizzard*—"we have each been supplied with a copy of it"— made one appearance only. It was Shackleton's answer to all those who were hurt because their contributions were not accepted for the *South Polar Times*. It was a bumper size, but the standard was much lower than the *South Polar Times*, and one issue was enough to ensure that there was no further demand for it.

3.5.02 Tremendous snow drift almost burying the ship. She is a perfect picture of winter now.

21.6.02 It is just six months today we left Lyttelton. The time is going away nicely. This is one of the days we have been looking forward to as it means that the sun will soon be on its way back again. Half of the dark nights have already gone. How nice it will be to get the sun again. This is midwinter here, so we are going to keep Christmas up on Monday 23rd. We are preparing for it now. The weather is very nice again today—hope it will keep like it.

22.6.02 Sunday. Everything quiet. Temperature very low but fine. Tomorrow will be our Christmas. We are going to dress up our messes for the occasion.

23.6.02 This seems rather a funny time to spend Christmas but we have celebrated ours today. We had a very nice time of it. A good dinner then plenty of singing which we kept up till about 1 o'clock. We also received Christmas cards by post from Ladies in England, also one from Admiral and Mrs Markham, and toys to play with. It of course is rather amusing to have toys and things down here, but it all helps to pass the time away. Mr Skelton took a photo of the messes by flashlight. The decorations were very good considering we have no evergreens.

25.6.02 Weather still very cold ($-47°$). Concert and sketch in the evening at Royal Terror Theatre. Audience and company not to exceed 46. Carriages at 9 p.m. It was a very successful evening altogether.

The next big event in the Royal Terror Theatre—the Hut ashore—was the anniversary of sailing from England: "Twelve months ago today we left England for Madeira. We have a nigger party to celebrate the event tonight in the Royal Terror Theatre."

The "nigger party" was a minstrel show dear to the hearts of all sailors at the time. The lectures in the evenings, at which attendance was voluntary, were on a much higher plane: "Mr Ferrar gave a lecture on geology and wireless telegraphy which was very interesting and helped to pass the evening away." There was, "Mr Hodgson on Biology and the wonders of the deep," and, a little later, "Captain been giving us a lecture on sledging tonight." "Lecture and magic lantern by Mr Armitage and Mr Skelton in the evening. Subject sledging with views of the Windwards Arctic expedition."

Lashly never missed anything of interest that was going on.

30.6.02 Twelve months today I joined the ship in London. What a difference in the scenery of today and that of last year. But the time is going along nicely. We are looking forward now for the return of the sun and also for news of those at home. I wonder how my wife and child is getting on. I am thinking that there will soon be some talk of a ship coming out to visit us. But of course that will be a long time yet. We have lots of work to do before we shall be able to get out of this place. Sledging parties will be leaving for different parts later, but it is too cold to start on any journey for some time to come.

7.7.02 Everybody is at work preparing for the sledge journeys which will soon be coming on now. We have plenty of work to do up to the present. There is no lack of work as yet in our department.

20.7.02 Sunday again. The weeks pass away very well. We are still in darkness, but there is hopes of getting light soon. It is partly light at midday. This is a very rough night again, but we have had a plus temperature again today. I suppose it is nice weather at home now and harvest is about commencing. Had a look at most of the photographs that have been taken since we left home. There is a good many of them and they are all very good on the whole. Some of them are very interesting to us as it brings back times that are gone.

CHAPTER 5

A WEATHER EYE

THE WEATHER AND natural phenomena were a constant source of interest and comment, particularly during the winter months when there was more time for reflection. For one whose duties lay mostly in the bowels of the ship his intelligent observations showed the countryman's instinct for all about him to a really remarkable degree.

11.4.02 We shall soon be losing the sun now. It will be rather dull then—nothing to warm us up and no light. It is a funny thing that when the wind blows the temperature rises, and a good thing too, or it would be bad for us as the wind is like the blast of a furnace. Frost bites are of frequent occurrence now. It is nothing to have your ear, nose, fingers or toes go, but it can be cured if taken in time.

17.4.02 Scientists out with dogs and sledges for Botanical and Geological specimens.

19.4.02 McMurdo Bay is still open sometimes. It freezes over then the wind springs up and blows it out to sea again.

23.4.02 Total eclipse of the moon at 5 a.m. but it was rather cloudy.

24.4.02 We lose the sun for four months today. This will of course be trying times, although we shall have some daylight for a little while yet. It is also getting colder. The average temperature is from 25° to 30° below zero.

1.5.02 This is the time to be home with all the glory of the summer coming on. How I should like to be there to go out for some nice walk with the dear ones at home. Of course we are always thinking of home and those that are there. It is now just over nine months since we left England. I do so hope everybody is keeping well, but of course we don't know. We are all in pretty good health. The time goes quickly with us. We have plenty to do to occupy our time at present. A concert was the programme last night.

23.5.02 The weather is much better. Quite a treat only minus 12, but the barometer is falling. We have the moon with us now which helps to make it a little lighter.

24.5.02 We sometimes get a good view of the Aurora Australis, but we should get better views if we were a little further north.

26.5.02 Mr Bernacchi registered earthquake shock.

29.5.02 Very cold day again. The temperature is minus 32°.

30.5.02 Well, this is a master place for change of temperature. Today the thermometer stands at 14° above zero. It do seem so nice. It is almost wonderful as the wind is blowing from the south, and a fairly stiff breeze. But if the wind gets towards the south it is always bitterly cold. This is on account of the barrier lying in that direction.

31.5.02 Weather very mild again today. Killed three seals. They are very plentiful here, only they don't get up on top of the ice unless the weather is warm. Fancy spring here where there is nothing growing or living above water, only us and the dogs as all the birds are gone north from here.

A note in the margin says the average temperature for the month of May was − 13°.

1.6.02 This is the Glorious First of June. Sunday routine as usual. Weather fairly mild, but dark. I daresay it is finer at home. The summer is drawing along in England now. We shall all be glad to have the sun coming south again.

6.6.02 Everything going on steady. Weather moderated a bit today. Very dark. No moon or sun. It really seems strange to continue dark so long.

9.6.02 We get some very good views of the Aurora Australis now. We are still groping about in the dark. One thing we still get plenty of work to do to help pass the time away, which is a good thing as it would be very trying with nothing whatever to do.

10.6.02 Weather very calm, but temperature – 38°. Plenty cold enough.

13.6.02 Mount Erebus was very active last night throwing up stuff.

14.6.02 This have been a splendid day. We have the moon a good part of the day which makes it better for getting about. Temperature is very low.

16.6.02 Blizzard blowing today. Temperature minus 8°, quite warm. Cannot get away from the ship the snow is so blinding.

17.6.02 The temperature went from – 42° to plus 11° last night.

18.6.02 We saw the moon and several mock moons surrounding it. Looked rather curious.

20.6.02 Lovely day. Had a game of football just to keep exercised a bit.

24.6.02 Temperature 47° below zero. This is the coldest we have had it up to the present.

27.6.02 Temperature went up to zero last night. Made it quite warm.

28.6.02 This is a most wonderful climate. The weather has been quite warm again today. Tonight it is blowing a gale, but not cold. It seems so curious that the temperature should rise with the wind, especially when blowing from the south.

This observation of Lashly's, that the temperature rose when the wind blew, was explained and confirmed many years later when a full Antarctic Meteorological report was published after the British Antarctic Expedition 1910–1913. Rapid radiation from the snow surface cools the air immediately above it forming a very cold layer near the ground. When the wind blows this layer is swept away and mixed with warmer air from above. It was the same next day:

29.6.02 Sunday. Very rough wind blowing at times, but not very cold, 10° below zero.

5.7.02 All quiet as usual. Nothing fresh to record. Most splendid Aurora last night that we have seen as yet.

6.7.02 We can see the twilight away in the north east at mid-day. A good sign that the sun is on her way back to us now.

10.7.02 Very rough again today and rather cold, but we don't feel it much now as we are getting used to it a bit of course. It is impossible to do much outdoor work in these temperatures.

18.7.02 The weather have changed but not, certainly, for the best. It is blowing a blizzard. This is a real peep at an antarctic winter. It is about the worst weather we have experienced up to the present, but again it is much warmer.

25.7.02 The ship is almost buried with snow. We have got rather a job with our boats. They are all buried under the snow. Hope we shall get them out all safe, but it will take up a good deal of time.

31.7.02 This is a dreadful night again. Can't hardly imagine such weather.

1.8.02 We had a very bad night last night. Mr Skelton and Mr Bernacchi were lost for about two hours coming from the hut to the ship. Lucky that some men and Mr Royds were coming over to the ship and heard them calling for help and went to their assistance. They were both frost bitten a bit, but it might have been a lot worse if the others had not heard them. It was impossible to see half a dozen yards before you.

4.8.02 We are getting a fair amount of wind, a thing we could well do without.

5.8.02 Very cold again. Forced to lay a bit low while it is like this.

7.8.02 Temperature very low, but no wind, 49·5° below zero on board the ship—the lowest we have registered on board as yet. A mile away from the ship at Cape Armitage it registered 77½ below, quite cold enough for anyone. We have got the moon back to help light us up.

9.8.02 Up to the present this is the coldest month we have had.

10.8.02 Went for a brisk walk at midday. Shall see the sun in about a fortnight now.

12.8.02 This have been a dreadful day again. We have had a tremendous blizzard blowing, but the temperature rose nearly up to zero.

17.8.02 A blizzard of the worst. The wind is from the south and it is not exactly cold, only minus 20°.

19.8.02 Fine all day but blizzard blowing again tonight. Quite frequent we get them this month. I hope it will get a little better when the sun comes back which will be on Saturday.

20.8.02 A very rough day this have been. Had it been fine, by going to the westward we should have been able to see the rim of the sun at midday. There is open water about five miles to the north of us.

22.8.02 The sun could be seen from the hill tops at midday.

23.8.02 A beautiful day, quite a treat. The sun have appeared now. 123 days we have been without it. Tomorrow we shall celebrate its return.

24.8.02 Sunday. Not a very pleasant day outdoors, but very comfortable on board. A good dinner and all enjoyed it.

He had to wait until the end of September before he could make a more hopeful entry about the weather.

28.9.02 It is still a good bit warmer. We had a plus temperature all last night, the first time this month. This have been the coldest month since our arrival here. We saw 46 Emperor Penguins going south this morning. This we are in hopes means warmer weather.

CHAPTER 6

FIRST SLEDGE TRIPS

27.8.02 FINE. BUSILY PREPARING for short sledge journeys next week, weather permitting.

31.8.02 Cold and rough all day. Busy preparing for sledge party leaving tomorrow. One party consisting of two officers and ten men going south as far as depot laid out last autumn. The other party made up of Captain, Scientist, Chief Engineer and Boatswain going towards Mount Erebus surveying. They are also taking a lot of dogs with them.

3.9.02 I am busily preparing to leave for a trip next week.

5.9.02 Both parties returned today having accomplished the work set out for them.

7.9.02 Sunday again. We are leaving on 10th for Mount Discovery. Shall probably be away for 14 days. It will be rather cold, but it is getting daylight now almost 12 hours a day. Snowing again today. Not at all nice weather for sledging. Too thick with drift and the snow is rather soft in places.

This western party was to see if there was a possible route inland up the Western Mountains by way of a huge glacier that could be seen to the south-west. The party was to be Lieutenant Royds, Dr Koettlitz, P.O. Evans, Leading Stoker Lashly, Leading Stoker Quartley and Able Seaman Wild. The combinations of Royds, Lashly, Quartley and Wild came to be known as the Guarantee Party, because they would guarantee to go anywhere and do anything. According to Scott the party "looked very workmanlike, and one could see at a glance the vast improvement that had been made since last year. The sledges were uniformly packed. Everything was in its right place and ready to hand, and all looked neat and businesslike. One shudders now to think of the slovenly manner in which we conducted things last autumn; at any rate, here is a first result of the care and attention of the winter."

The sledging rations had been the subject of considerable thought and experiment. Lashly made a careful list of the provisions and how they were to be divided up for the three inmates of each tent. It is given below, with the last column—the ration in ounces—as given by Scott in *Voyage of the Discovery.*

Article	Weekly Allowance per tent	Daily Allowance	Ounces per day
Biscuit	½ case	4 biscuits	12·0
Oatmeal	3 lbs	12 spoonfuls	1·5
Pemmican	10 lbs	Just under 1½ lbs	7·6
Red Ration	1½ lbs	6 spoonfuls	1·1
Plasmon	No mention in the diary		2·0
Pea soup	1 lb	3 spoonfuls	1·5
Cheese	2 lbs		2·0
Chocolate	1½ lbs		1·1
Cocoa	1 lb	4½ spoonfuls	0·7
Sugar	5 lbs	63 lumps	3·8
Tea	3 × 1 lb tins for 6 men for two weeks		¾ lbs a tent } per week
Marmalade	4 lbs		
Grated cheese	1 lb		
Onion powder	½ lb	per week	½ lb per tent per week

Article	*Weekly Allowance per tent*	*Daily Allowance*	*Ounces per day*
Pepper	¾ lb	Tin last 3 weeks	¼ lb per tent per week
Salt	½ lb	Two weeks	·4 lb per tent per week
Celery Seed		Whole trip	

In addition there was one gallon of paraffin and half a pint of spirit for each ten days. Pemmican was the finest dried lean beef ground to a powder and mixed with 60 per cent beef fat. It was used as thick soup, stiffened with biscuit, and it made "hoosh"— the staple diet of Antarctic travellers. The Red ration, a compound of bacon and pea flour, was also used to thicken the hoosh. The whole daily ration made about 29 ozs of food value after the water content was lost.

This was to be Lashly's first sledge trip and he went into some detail of the procedure that later became so familiar to him.

10.9.02 We left the ship at 10.50 for the purpose of trying to discover a passage through the western mountains to the magnetic pole, also to look for a passage to the south between the islands. It is rather early for sledging, as we all know, but the Captain seems to think it necessary to commence as soon as possible. So we left the ship with 14 days provisions, sleeping and camping equipment, the party consisting of six all told with two sledges. Lieutenant Royds, Dr Koettlitz myself in one tent, with three other men in another—Quartley, Evans and Wild. The temperature on leaving the ship being 33° below zero we, of course, made very good headway, halting after about 4 miles out for lunch which consisted of biscuits and cheese. We then started again and kept up a good pace until about 5 o'clock when we camped for the night. First of all up tent, then get cookers ready and start the evening meal, which we all very much enjoyed after the first day's tramp. The meal consisted of American pemmican, red ration, plasmon, and different kinds of soup with biscuit and tea. It don't take very long to get these things ready as the primus lamp very soon fetches the water to boiling pitch. The foods are easily cooked, pretty well all of them being concentrated. As soon as the meal is over there is nothing to be done but clear out the gear for the sleeping bags to be brought in, and then turn in. This is the worst part of sledging—nights, specially in such low temperatures as we are experiencing the first night out 48° below zero is a little below the ordinary sledging done before. The night is long and you are glad to get up and get breakfast, pack up and be off for the day. It is all right while you are on the move, but during the long hours of the night it is bad to be shivering, and no sleep whatever.

11.9.02 We were under way again about 9 this morning in a still low temperature, but no wind. A fog began to come on in the evening. We were now getting in to rather rough bad ice, one or other of us continually going through. But we pushed on till 5 o'clock when we camped again for the night with the same routine. The temperature being 45° below, we turned in with the prospect of another very cold night. We found in the morning the thermometer had gone as low as 57°. Quite cold enough for any of us.

12.9.02 Another cold foggy day. We could not see exactly where we were all day, but we had got into some very uneven and hummocky ice. It was very heavy pulling, the sledges continually going over. We were forced to have one man to hold up the sledge while the others dragged the loads over it. But the farther we went the worse the ice got.

It is a splendid sight to be amongst it here—the hummocks all kinds of shapes and forms and range from six to thirty feet high. It forms a good shelter from the wind. Between the hummocks there are long channels of nice smooth ice like rivers of fresh water frozen over. It is a beautiful sight and well worth seeing. It would be a study to know how it gets like it, and also how long it takes, but it must be an enormous amount of years to get in such a state.

13.9.02 We made our way out of the ice that is so rough. Very low temperatures.

14.9.02 Sunday. Got out of the bad travelling at noon and halted for lunch. We experienced beautiful weather today. Did not pitch tents for lunch but made our tea out in the open in a temperature of 42° below zero. It don't seem hardly creditable, but it is a fact.

15.9.02 Made very good headway today travelling over very hard but rough ice, halting in the evening between two islands, but not in a very sheltered position.

16.9.02 Got under way in pretty good time, but it was heavy pulling all the morning. Cleared up a bit at midday. We halted for lunch at 1 p.m. and about 1.30 a blizzard came on us all of a sudden compelling us to secure our tents and prepare for a rough time of it. The other tent blew down, but we managed to get it up again after a struggle, and during the struggle my sleeping bag blew away, which was very bad for me. But there was a way of getting over this difficulty as the other tent had a 3-man bag, so we made a four-man bag of it, but it was rather crowded.

The line of thought on sleeping bags was still in the experimental stage. Some believed that a 3-man bag would give extra warmth, while others believed that the additional comfort of a single bag would compensate for any increased cold. The question of saving weight also made a 3-man bag desirable, but later expeditions always used single bags, supporting the theory that personal convenience was more important.

This same blizzard forced Scott, who was leading one of the other parties, to return to the ship. Scott woke up during the blizzard in the night to find he had rolled out of the tent in his sleeping bag and was lying in the open. They were always careful after this to stack enough snow blocks on the tent valances to hold them down firmly.

17.9.02 The blizzard is over, but very low temperature. Can't see anything of my bag, but might find it on our way back. We are going to return as we think it safest. We could only go on one more day. Came across my bag at night about 8 miles from where it started. Should be a little better off for room tonight. Made excellent progress today—about 25 miles. Met Captain, Mr Barne and Mr Shackleton about 15 miles from ship going out. We shall reach the ship to-morrow if the weather is fine.

They did not travel at all on the next day, Thursday 18th as Lashly explained.

18.9.02 After having a very stiff day of it yesterday we turned in our bags at a very low temperature at 8 p.m. and soon after a blizzard began to scour the place, but it got a little warmer during the night. In the morning the wind was as bad as ever so we had to stay on in our sleeping bags which we could not leave until about 12 a.m. on Friday morning. We were all the time without food or drink except for a little piece of chocolate and biscuit.

19.9.02 As soon as we could stir we dug our sledges out and prepared ourselves a meal which was completed and the sledges packed by 2 a.m. We made our way to the ship after being away 10 days in as low temperature as man has ever been sledging in. Leaving our last camp the temperature was 53° below zero—quite cold enough for any human being. After leaving camp we trudged along pretty well over rather soft snow until 8 a.m.—a distance of about 9 miles when we reached the ship in time for breakfast. Some of the men and Mr Skelton came out to give us a pull in. The Captain's party returned in the afternoon. Mr Armitage and party are still away but we don't expect them before next week.

20.9.02 Saturday. Had a good rest and feel a lot better for it. Did not get any frost bites, but the tips of fingers are very tender.

21.9.02 Sunday. A very nice day, still resting ready for our next journey.

22.9.02 Carrying on as usual. Still very cold.

24.9.02 Captain, Mr Shackleton and Boatswain left ship again today for another trip. Also Dr Koettlitz, Mr Bernacchi and the carpenter going south-west where we discovered some very interesting things but could not stay as we had to try and discover the southern passage for laying the depot.

25.9.02 No sign of Mr Armitage's party yet.

26.9.02 Mr Armitage and party arrived at 6 this morning after a rough time and a long march. Although they did not get as low temperatures as us they had a rough time and were away 15 days.

Three members of this party were in a state of collapse due to scurvy. An immediate examination of all on board revealed that there were signs of scurvy in a good many others as well. So the issue of tinned food was forbidden and the stock of fresh seal meat was replenished. The outbreak was soon under control, but it was not the last that was to be heard of this age-old scourge of seafaring people who lacked adequate quantities of fresh food. The "Guarantee Party" were all found to be in first class condition, and, after a spell of fine weather, they set off again on 4th October. Skelton and Petty Officer Evans were the other members of the party which was to go to Cape Crozier to leave the messages they had tried to take on the autumn journey in March.

3.10.02 All quiet as usual. Captain and party returned tonight We leave tomorrow all being well. Hope it will be warmer than last trip.

This hope was not fulfilled.

4.10.02 Left ship at 11 a.m. on ski. Temperature minus 15°. Distance made good 5½ miles geographical. We travelled first and last hour on ski.

5.10.02 Travelling on ski as the snow is very soft. Made 6½ miles, good.

6.10.02 Still heavy going and low temperature to contend with. It has been below −40° every night as yet.

7.10.02 Weather fine but cold and snow very soft.

8.10.02 Same as yesterday. Good view of Mount Erebus.

9.10.02 Still very cold. Last night we registered 58·5° below, about the lowest temperature ever registered while anyone has been out sledging.

10.10.02 We arrived at the Knoll at 9 p.m. after a very hard day's work. We are in a pass about 1000 feet above sea level. The Ross Sea is frozen over as far as we can see. We are about 4½ miles from Cape Crozier.

11.10.02 Mr Skelton and Evans started off on foot to deliver the despatches which they accomplished and returned to the camp at 6 p.m. We stayed behind and built a snow wall round the camp.

12.10.02 Sunday: Could not do much today on account of the weather. Had early supper and turned in. A blizzard started about 6 o'clock.

13, 14, 15, 16 and 17th October: Now comes the hour of our hardship which lasted longer than any of us expected. We were confined to the tent for five days and nights while the storm lasted. A time none of us would care to live over again. We were no doubt saved by the snow wall from being blown away altogether. The tent was completely buried with snow which made it very uncomfortable as the tent was pushed in upon us so that we had no room to move. We were in a very cramped condition. On the Tuesday morning the storm lulled for about half an hour when we managed to get out and get our cooker and have a warm meal after lying waiting for it since Sunday night. Of course, a warm meal means a good deal when you are lying in a temperature from 15° to 20° below, but we had only had time to just get it ready before the blizzard continued with increased force. It compelled us to lie low till Friday before we could get out and get more food to cook. We had biscuit, sugar, Bovril and chocolate to live on, but it was a treat to get something warm. We managed after the wind ceased to get away at 6 a.m. on Saturday 18th.

Scott added the information that the space inside the tents during this blizzard was so reduced by the weight of snow pressing down that the occupants were forced to lie with knees bent double. They could hardly turn from side to side and suffered martyrdom from cramp. He thought it was due to the snow walls round the camp that the drift had been able to build up to this extent. But even an experience like this could not damp Lashly's ardour for probing the secrets of the great unknown.

18.10.02 Turned out to be a very nice day. We got down into the valley and pitched our camp again. Mr Skelton, Quartley, and Evans going to the end of the barrier with difficulty for the purpose of photographing the junction with the land. There they discovered an Emperor Penguin rookery of which Mr Skelton got some very nice photographs. It is a thing that has never been seen before, so it will be very interesting to naturalists. We brought back some young ones. Mr Royds, myself, and Wild remained behind and went to the hummock and ridges to try to ascertain the cause of them. The ice is thrown up about 20 to 50 feet high by the pressure, which is immense, of the ice and snow coming down from the slope of Mount Terror and pushing up against the barrier. The ridges are running from towards the south-west for some miles, and gradually curving round towards the slope of Mount Erebus.

19.10.02 This has been a very nice day. Temperature rather low, but no wind makes it warm. This is the sixth anniversary of my wedding day. What changes time brings in people's lives. We are now on our way to the ship again, but have got to follow the ridges as far as possible.

23.10.02 Mr Skelton and Mr Royds have been suffering from snow blindness. We shall reach the ship on Friday all being well. I have got snow blindness in my right eye.

24.10.02 We are back on board after 21 days absence. A blizzard came on before we reached the ship. Some came out to meet us.

CHAPTER 7

PREPARING FOR SEA

29.10.02 THE CAPTAIN WILL leave on 31st all being well
with dogs for his farthest south. My eye is not well yet.

2.11.02 Captain Scott, Dr Wilson and Mr Shackleton left ship
at 10 a.m. with 18 dogs, all hands turning out to send them
off. It is to be hoped they will have a pleasant and successful
trip and come back safe.

3.11.02 Three officers and six men left ship today, some going
north and some east. There are only 24 of us left in the ship
now—quite a small party. We have been living on seal for
nearly a month now. Rather rough weather but we have got
the midnight sun for another four months.

4.11.02 The weather is improving every day.

7.11.02 We are preparing to celebrate the King's birthday
tomorrow.

8.11.02 It have been a fairly fine day but not so good as could
have been. But we have enjoyed ourselves very well with
sports and a jolly good feed. The evening being spent by
magic lantern and a concert. Prizes distributed afterwards.

9.11.02 Sunday. Had a good lay in, but, the weather being fine,
had to get out for a walk.

14.11.02 All quiet. Very nice weather prevails.

15.11.02 Finished up the sports. Had a concert in the evening.

18.11.02 Mr Royds returned from Cape Crozier penguin
rookery. Captured one Emperor Penguin egg. This is the
first and only specimen that is about.

23.11.02 Sunday. Southern depot party returned today, having left Captain and party in Latitude 79° 15 with the appearance of making a good journey south as the passage looked clear for miles. This is farther south than anyone have been before.

29.11.02 Western party left today, 21 all told. Mr Armitage in charge with Mr Skelton as second but 9 return in about 17 days leaving 12 to go on to the magnetic pole these returning at the end of January. There are only about 20 of us on board now. We have plenty of work to do. No one can be idle the weather is good and health of all hands good. We shall prepare the ship for sea now.

One of the first jobs to be done was to dig out the boats. They had all been hoisted out and left on the ice to make more room on deck, but the weight of snow on them had forced them into the ice where they were well and truly frozen in.

9.12.02 Rescued one of the boats from a watery grave after being buried for the last 8 months. There are still four more to come if they can be got out. Warmest day since arrival, temperature 37·5°.

28.12.02 Much finer. Supplementary party returned from the west at 8 p.m.

21.12.02 Twelve months ago we left Lyttelton. The time have passed very well. We shall be looking for open water and the relief ship in another month from now.

25.12.02 Christmas day. A quiet time but enjoyed ourselves.

27.12.02 Work is the order of the day, we are very busy preparing the boilers and engines for a move when the time comes.

28.12.02 Sunday. The last we are going to keep up as there is so much to do at present and so few to do it. We are all looking forward to the ice breaking up.

31.12.02 This is the last of the old year. It have passed away quickly. One can hardly realize it is more than a year ago we left New Zealand.

1.1.03 Today we commenced the new year in glorious weather, thinking of those at home. Another party of three left today for the south for a fortnight. This will probably be the last party to leave this season.

6.1.03 No sign of the ice breaking up near the ship yet. We have been busy these two days melting ice for the main boilers. Worked till 10 both nights. Weather being splendid all the time.

11.1.03 Sunday. Got out another boat today. We don't get any Sunday now. Work every day.

15.1.03 All the boats are out now. Some of them are a bit damaged.

18.1.03 Lit one of the main boilers today ready for melting ice for ship's tanks.

19.1.03 Commenced melting ice at 6 o'clock this morning. Melted 20 tons, finished at 8 o'clock. Mr Armitage and Mr Skelton returned at night after 52 days absence with all well except one man, he not being able to stick the long drag very well. A very good record was made, 377 miles out and back, 9,000 feet altitude attained.

21.1.03 Working as hard as we can to get the ship ready for sea.

23.1.03 Myself and the boatswain on the look out for the relief ship on the hill this morning, and fancied we saw the smoke from her over a glacier at the foot of Mount Erebus.

24.1.03 This is a glorious day. The relief ship was sighted at midnight last, so we are going on a sledge trip at 10 this morning as she cannot get within 8 miles of us yet. Lieutenant Armitage, Mr Skelton, Mr Hodgson, Mr Bernacchi and myself going with 8 others.

25.1.03 (Sunday) On arriving within a mile and a half of the

Morning (relief ship) we had to proceed with the greatest care, the ice being very unsafe, several going through. The Captain of the *Morning* came to meet us and we scrambled on board at 5 in the evening. Very glad to exchange greetings and hear the news. We got our letters, at least the latest ones, and, of course, were glad to hear the good news from all at home. The worst of it was the ice got in such bad condition that we could not return until Monday night with the other men's letters, and then at great risk, only some of us returning.

30.1.03 Mr Barne and party have returned after 43 days absence. This only leaves the Captain and party out of the ship now.

31.1.03 Mr Royds, Mr Barne, Dr Koettlitz and Mr Dellbridge with eight men left today for the *Morning* to fetch parcels and papers for us.

1.2.03 Sunday. Party came back from the relief ship with more parcels for all hands. No sign of the ice breaking up yet.

3.2.03 Party gone down to the *Morning* again today. Captain sighted about 10 miles off tonight.

4.2.03 Mr Skelton and Mr Bernacchi went out to meet the Captain and party. They arrived at the ship about 4.30 p.m. dragging their load. The Captain and Dr Wilson looking very well although they were done up. They had to pull all the lot as Mr Shackleton was ill and could only manage to walk. Another thing—the dogs all died a month previous which made it very hard for them. The farthest point south was 82° 17'. We dressed and manned ship for the occasion. Captain Colbeck and a party from the *Morning* arrived soon after and we had a good time at night.

Scott's party had turned north on 31st December, but Wilson had been observing signs of scurvy developing in Shackleton for a fortnight before that. They were all suffering from extreme hunger. The dogs had never pulled their weight on the trip and were killed off one by one to be fed to the others. The last dog had been killed on 15th January. By the time the party reached their last depot on 28th January, Scott and Wilson were also showing symptoms of scurvy and their hunger was acute. With no need to conserve food they succumbed to an orgy of over-eating which cost them a sleepless night and agonies of indigestion.

5.2.03 Everything quiet as usual. Not much doing today. Party gone back to the *Morning* tonight.

8.2.03 One year today we arrived here and there is no sign of the ice breaking away yet. It is quite possible we may have to winter here again, although there is time yet.

10th to 24th. Daily bringing stores from the relief ship weather permitting. Ship landing coal on glacier for us if we should happen to get free this year. We have had to get the stores a distance of 6 miles. Some of our people are leaving us in the relief ship to go home. One or two invalids, altogether one Officer and eight men.

Shackleton, who was unfit, was the Officer returning, much against his will. The men were all volunteers. When Scott decided to reduce numbers against the probability of spending a second winter in the ice, he outlined his proposals to the men and called for eight volunteers. A list was sent round and Scott wrote: "The result is curiously satisfactory. There are eight names on the list, and not only that, but these names are precisely those which I should have placed there had I undertaken the selection myself. As regards the messdeck, therefore, we shall be left with the pick of our company, all on good terms, and all ready, as they say, to stand by the ship whatever betides. With such an uncertain future before us, it is good to feel that there is not a single soul to mar the harmony of our relations, and to know that, whatever may befall, one can have complete confidence in one's companions."

28.2.03 Weather very unsettled. Still fetching stores from the *Morning*. She is leaving on Monday.

1.3.03 Nearly all hands gone to the relief ship to see her off.

2.3.03 *Morning* left at 2 p.m. today for New Zealand. We may get out this year but it is doubtful.

3rd to 22.3.03 We are beginning to be settled down for another winter as the ice don't seem as if it will go out now. The temperature is very low as compared to last year at the corresponding time. We have taken in seal meat and skua gulls for the winter, and have dismantled the engines again.

With no new experiences to report as he slipped into winter routine again Lashly made briefer entries in his diary. Dull periods were bracketed together, but nothing of interest was allowed to pass unnoticed. At the end of March he declared: "I don't think there is much chance of our getting out this year now, as the sea is frozen over again out towards the north."

1.4.03 Have taken up hockey as a pastime and exercise. We play a match every afternoon. We are thinking the *Morning* is back in New Zealand. How we should have liked to have been back there now just for a change. The worst time of the year is just coming on. In three weeks time we shall lose the sun, then for the darkness. But we shall be all right as long as we continue in good health.

2.4.03 Work is getting slack. Nearly done all there is to do this season. Commence winter routine soon now.

3.4.03 Weather fine but cold. Played hockey again today. Temperature $-16°$

H.M.S. *Discovery* in her winter quarters (*Royal Geographical Soc.*)

Ships at anchor in Robertson Bay (*Royal Geographic Soc.*)

5.4.03 Still cold with strong easterly wind. Temperature $-15°$. Minus 25° at Cape Armitage.

12.4.03 Easter Sunday. Service as usual.

16/17.4.03 Exercise both days, hockey. We lose the sun on 21st, two days earlier than last year. Shall be glad when the time comes for its return. We are continually registering 30° and 40° below.

23.4.03 The sun has left us but we can see it shining on the mountain tops.

26.4.03 Sunday routine as usual. Very low temperature we are getting now. We have fitted up the acetylene gas on the messdeck. It makes things a bit lighter.

30.4.03 Finished playing hockey. It is too dark for outdoor games now.

14.5.03 The temperature is very low, $-52·5°$. At Cape Armitage the lowest was $-67·5°$, a record 99·7° of frost. We have also had five days complete calm.

15.5.03 The temperature have gone up by leaps and bounds with a good breeze.

20.5.03 We are in for more wind. The temperature has gone from $-47°$ to plus 2° in less than 24 hours. This, according to last year's observations, means wind and plenty of it.

21.5.03 We are getting plenty of wind, but not too bad to get out in.

30.5.03 Have not wrote anything lately. It is colder this year than last, but we are not having so much blizzard.

There was only one entry to cover the whole of June: "This is the month we are looking for the sun to begin its course back to us. Kept up Christmas on 22nd and had a very good time altogether. The health of all hands is still good. Nothing better could be desired."

5.7.03 Sunday. We carry on quietly every day as usual. Temperature is very low again 48° below. In fact the last few days have been some of the coldest since our arrival here. Wind varying from force 6 to 10, with the temperature from 30 to 40 below. It is a job to stick it when it is like this. We are busy preparing for sledging later on.

All the sledging gear was refitted during the winter and plans were laid for the next sledging season. On 23rd August Lashly noted that, "All our fresh mutton goes today, so we have only seal to live on for the next four or five months," and then he went on to list the various sledge journeys that were to come. The ones with which he was concerned were a three week depot-laying trip to the Western mountains starting on 9th September, to be followed by a much longer trip—about 55 days—over these same mountains on to the Victoria Land Plateau. All sledge parties were due back in the ship by 15th December so that all efforts could be turned to freeing her for relief in January, 1904. The sledging programme required the supporting parties from the major journeys to get back to the ship by 15th November in order to set up and provision a "sawing camp" on the ice. It was planned to saw a channel from the ship to the sea if the ice showed no signs of breaking up.

The only dogs left at this time were eight survivors of the litters born the previous year, so they were little more than puppies and their use was not contemplated on any of this season's journeys. Indeed, Scott never used dogs again on a major sledge journey unless they could get safely back to their base. Any repetition of the plan used on his southern journey, which had necessitated killing dogs for food, appalled him. He wrote in his report: "This method of using dogs is one which can only be adopted with reluctance. One cannot calmly contemplate the murder of animals which possess such intelligence and individuality, which have frequently such endearing qualities and which very possibly one has learnt to regard as friends and companions. In my mind no journey ever made with dogs can approach the height of that fine conception which is realized when a party of men go forth to face hardships, dangers and difficulties with their own unaided efforts and by days and weeks of hard physical labour succeed in solving some problem of the great unknown. Surely in this case the conquest is more nobly and splendidly won."

From this date Scott never made a major sledge journey without Lashly and Evans in his party.

CHAPTER 8

THE WESTERN JOURNEY

THE WESTERN DEPOT laying party got away on 9th September to lay their depot on the Ferrar Glacier. Apart from the cold it was an uneventful trip and Lashly contented himself with giving a meteorological summary in his diary. The depot was left in the middle of the glacier stream under the Cathedral Rocks. Just two observations on a novel sledging technique and unusual conditions occur:

9.9.03 We left the ship at 10.45 with a strong wind behind us. Proceeded on ski for a few miles with sail set until about 3 p.m. when the wind dropped.

12.9.03 Minimum during the night − 36·5°. Started at 9 a.m. Fine morning, strong mirage all the day. Occasional light breezes but generally calm. Camped at six. The sledges pulling rather heavy on account of frost crystals on the surface.

When this happened, always in very cold weather, the snow became more the consistency of sand and the sledges would not glide at all.

They got back to the ship at midnight on 20th September and Lashly summed up: "Our trip on the whole was accomplished in rather good time under the circumstances. Because of the low temperature we had very heavy hauling all the time, we were all glad to get back for a comfortable night doss." He gave a list of the achievements:

Days out inclusive	12 days
Days on march	11·3 days
Distance covered	140 miles (geographical)
Height reached	2,000 ft above sea level
Average daily march	12·4 miles (for whole trip)

Return journey accomplished in 3½ days.

distance covered 70 miles, average daily 20 miles

Total weight on leaving ship	1,080 lbs
Total weight per man	180 lbs
Weight of gear left at Depot	430 lbs
Weight on returning to ship	521 lbs
Increase of weight of gear due to moisture, ice, etc.	81·5 lbs

11.10.03 Sunday again. The last we expect to do on board until 15th December. We leave tomorrow for the west, Captain, Mr Skelton, Boatswain, myself, Evans, Handsley, with Mr Ferrar, Carpenter, Plumley, Williamson, Weller, Kennar. Our party to be away 9 weeks, Mr Ferrar with two hands 7 weeks, and the Carpenter 5 weeks with the other two. Mr Ferrar's party acting as supporting party to us.

The advance party had been selected by Scott with the "greatest care", and they set off on 12th October: "As I had determined that from first to last of this trip there should be hard marching, we stretched across over the 45 miles to New Harbour at a good round pace, and by working long hours succeeded in reaching the snow cape on the near side early on 14th—a highly creditable performance with such heavy loads." By 18th October they were making their way up the glacier and had reached a height of 6,000 feet. The sledges had had a rough passage across hard weather beaten ice, and the moraine of the glacier, and the runners had become torn and split. Three out of the four were almost useless and there was nothing for it but to return to the ship for repairs and replacements. "Heaven knows what sacrifice of time we shall have to make," wrote Scott, "however, there shall not be more than I can help, and things which have gone fast in the past, will positively have to fly in the future."

On the following days they came as near flying as possible. There were 87 miles to cover back to the ship with three broken-down sledges. By the evening of the 19th they had covered 27 miles and were back at sea level. The next day, which included an hour's halt to strip the torn metal off the sledge runners, they made 24 miles. They reached the ship on 21st October after pulling 36 miles in the day.

Lashly had written nothing else until they got back to the ship when his only comment was:

22.10.03 Had to return to the ship on account of the sledges having the German silver all worn off the runners.

26.10.03 Left the ship at 10.30 a.m. Hope we shall have better luck with the sledges this time. Done about 22 miles. Only 9 of us this time. Carpenter, one stoker and one bluejacket left on board.

Repairs completed they were back on the glacier on 27th October, averaging 25 miles a day. They tried fitting under runners to preserve the sledges, but these broke up and had to be discarded: "Had to stop after lunch and take off the under-runners, all broke up." But worse trouble was in store. On reaching the depot once more they found the lid of the instrument box had been blown off. In addition to one or two small articles, Scott found his "Hints to Travellers" was missing. This was the book containing the tables that were necessary for working out sun sights to establish their position when they got on to the featureless plateau. He was determined not to return to the ship again, and, with the agreement of the rest of the party, he decided to press on without the tables. The sledges were still giving trouble.

1.11.03 Started this morning at 7 a.m. Packed sledges and left one weeks provisions for return journey. Served out 5 days food. We have now got 6 weeks and 6 days food with us. We shall be dragging about 230 lbs a man. Had to camp early and repair the German silver or we shall never reach the top with a sound sledge.

"Each difficulty only serves to show more clearly their resourcefulness," wrote Scott. "This particular trouble has called on the metal workers, and no sooner had we halted and unpacked the sledges than Skelton and Lashly were hard at work with pliers, files and hammers stripping off the torn metal and lapping fresh pieces over the weak places. They have established a little workshop in this wild spot, and for hours the scrape of the file and the tap of the hammer have feebly broken the vast silence. We have hopes of the lapping process which is now being effected, but it needs very careful fitting; each separate piece of metal protection is made to overlap the piece behind it, like slates on a roof! I should doubt whether such work could be done by people unaccustomed to dealing with these matters."

2.11.03 Started again after finishing repairs. It increased to a gale at lunch and we had great difficulty finding a camping ground it being all bare blue ice about here. Finally we made for the land and camped, all continually getting frost-bitten.

3.11.03 The sun shone out quite hot at lunch. We started to climb a cascade with one sledge at a time, but it was so dangerous the Captain decided to try another place where we succeeded fairly easy, although it was very heavy dragging and our sledges are getting shaky on it.

4.11.03 Made another start. A fine morning but it did not last long. It came on to blow a gale much to our discomfort. The temperature going down to minus 20° plenty of frost bites. We had great difficulty in finding a camping ground it being all bare blue ice round here. Experienced rather a rough time getting the tents up. Had dinner at 7 and turned in for the day.

5.11.03 Still blowing and drifting. Mr Skelton and myself taking off German silver from the runners of the sledges, not a very pleasant job. The wind went down for a little while, but soon increased again worse than ever.

This blizzard raged for a whole week, and while it lasted they were forced to spend 22 out of 24 hours in their sleeping bags. "Things are looking serious," wrote Scott, "I fear the long spell of bad weather is telling on us. The cheerfulness of the party is slowly waning; I heard the usual song from Lashly this morning, but it was very short-lived and dolorous." They got away again on 11th November, and reached the plateau on 13th.

14.11.03 Got to the top on to the inland ice cap. We are now about 9,300 feet above sea level. Mr Ferrar and party we left on 11th, they going back down the glacier for geological research.

They plodded westward and Lashly reported: "Not much land in sight now." "Dragging heavy." "Surface bad", occurs with depressing frequency. Then they had to resort to relay work—taking half the load on and going back for the other half.

20.11.03 Dragging getting worse. Handstey's chest and throat gave out. Had to do relay work, this the Captain can't stand.

21.11.03 Started on relay work again today. This is not making much progress.

22.11.03 Have decided to go on to lunch with both sledges. After, Captain, myself and Evans going on for a few days more. The other three returning to the ship. They gave us a pull out for two or three miles and then said goodbye.

Scott decided to send half the party back under Skelton's leadership. He went on with Lashly and Evans. "From the date on which, so reluctantly, I decided that some of my party should turn homeward, there followed, for us who remained, three weeks of the hardest physical work that I have ever experienced, and yet three weeks on which I can but look with unmixed satisfaction, for I do not think it would have been possible to have accomplished more in the time. I have little wonder when I remember the splendid qualities and physique of the two men who remained with me by such a severe process of selection. With these two men behind me our sledge seemed to become a living thing, and the days of slow progress were numbered. We took the rough and the smooth alike, working patiently on through the long hours with scarce a word and never a halt between meal and meal. Troubles and discomforts were many, and we could only guess at the progress we made, but we knew that by sticking to our task we should have our reward when our observations came to be worked out on board the ship.

"There is no class of men so eminently adapted by training to cope with the troubles and tricks of sledging life as sailors," Scott wrote. "One would have to search far for a better sledge companion than the British Bluejacket." This had not been Nansen's experience on his sledge journey across the North Polar Ice in 1895. As soon as he left his ship, the *Fram*, Nansen regretted his choice of a sailor companion. This was a man called Johanssen who was a thoroughly competent seaman and a fine athlete, but who was unable to give Nansen any sort of intellectual companionship. Scott, who knew Nansen, must have been alive to this situation and would not have chosen Lashly and Evans only for their practical value. Being a naval officer to the core he had more in common with his sailors than Nansen the scientist had, even so, the social and educational gulf between senior officer and lower deck was very great. In all his accounts of events on this journey Scott never used the word "I", it is always "we". They even shared a three-man sleeping bag. Scott, who was a thinking man, found the companionship of Lashly and Evans stimulating and congenial. A very real bond of affection and loyalty existed between the three men.

24.11.03 Started as usual but soon got on a worse surface than ever. The wind seems to be very troublesome here and the snow is cut about a good deal, leaving what is termed as sastragi.

30.11.03 Everything have been unchanged for the last 4 or 5 days. This is our last day out. Tomorrow we make our return journey to the ship. We are about 300 miles from the ship now. We have 19 days provisions and about 16 days oil for our journey back to the glacier where we have got 10 days more food and oil.

As they turned for home Scott wrote in his diary: "We are all very proud of our march out. I don't know where we are, but I know we must be a long way to the west from my rough noon observation of the compass variation; besides which we cannot have marched so many hours without covering a long distance. We have been discussing this matter at supper, and wondering whether future explorers will travel further over this inhospitable country. Evans remarked that if they did they 'would have to leg it', and indeed I think they would."

1.12.03 Started as usual but on the homeward track. The sledge is still dragging very heavy. Although we get lighter with our load it don't make any difference to the pulling. We are all glad when night comes. After pulling for 9½ hours we are quite tired and hungry. We all of us would like more food, but we can't carry more. Breakfast consists of one biscuit, a pot of Pemmican oatmeal, red ration, a little seal meat, onion powder, and plasmon mixed, and a cup of tea with plasmon and a little sugar in. We then go for about five hours and stop to lunch which consists of a little cheese and one and a half biscuits, a cup of tea and half a stick of chocolate. We then go for another 4½ hours and camp and prepare dinner which consists of nearly the same as breakfast. But instead of oatmeal we use Symingtons pea soup. This meal we make a little bigger—1½ biscuits—and cocoa comes in place of tea. We now get the bag in and prepare for a good night's sleep after a good day's work.

2nd to 6th December. Everything going on as usual but we have had a very bad light to travel by. One day we had to camp as the fog was so thick we could not see a foot in front of us.

On 2nd December, Scott estimated that they were 17 marches from the glacier. There were just over 14 days' full rations left and about 12 days' allowance of oil. "Luckily the gloom of the outer world has not been allowed to enter the door of our tent. My companions spare no time for solemn thought; they are invariably cheerful and busy. Few of our camping hours go by without a laugh from Evans and a song from Lashly. I have not quite penetrated the latter yet; there is only one verse, which is about the plucking of a rose. It can scarcely be called a finished musical performance, but I should miss it much if it ceased." Later he wrote, "My companions are undefeatable. However tiresome our day's march or however gloomy the outlook, they always find something to jest about. In the evenings we have long arguments about Naval matters, and generally agree that we could rule that service a great deal better than any Board of Admiralty. Incidentally, I learn a great deal about lower deck life—more than I could hope to have done under ordinary conditions."

7.12.03 It has been clear nearly all day today. We have caught a glimpse of the land running away to the south-west. A good sign that we are making good progress. We were visited by two skua gulls, rather a long way inland for them to be.

8th to 12th December. We have been struggling along very much in the fog, not knowing exactly where we were. And we have also been on cold tea, cold lunch, and cold cocoa at night as our oil is getting short and we want to try and make it run out with the food.

Entries in Scott's diary over this period included: "Evans and Lashly have both been suffering a good deal from cold feet and fingers; my feet keep well though fingers easily go." "I am a little alarmed about our oil, so have decided to march half an hour extra each night." "None of us seems to want much sleep." The shortage of oil was caused partly by seepage. The corks or bungs in the oil tins could not be made to fit tightly when they were subjected to very low temperatures. Different methods of corking were tried, but none was satisfactory. The problem was still not solved ten years later, with much more serious consequences then.

"Hunger is growing upon us once more," Scott wrote, "though not to such an alarming extent as it did last year; still, we practise the same device for serving out our rations, and are as keen at picking up the scraps as ever." Shackleton had invented an ingenious scheme for ensuring fair shares of "hoosh" which eliminated all suspicion of cheating. The cook divided it out while one of the others turned his head away. Holding up a portion the cook asked him, "Whose is this?" and it was given to the person named. "I think Evans idea of joy is pork," Scott went on. "Whilst Lashly dreams of vegetables, and especially apples. He tells us stories of his youth when these things, and not much else, were plentiful." On 9th December the surface was bad again and their advance was reduced to about one mile an hour. "I have done some hard pulling, but never anything to equal this," wrote Scott. "This afternoon the surface grew worse and worse, and at the end of the march we were all dog tired. The state of affairs is again serious . . . we have had a long discussion about matters tonight. I told the men I thought we were in a pretty tight place, and that we should have to take steps accordingly. I proposed that we should increase our marching hours by one hour, go on half allowance of oil, and if we don't sight landmarks in a couple of days reduce our rations. I explained the scheme for oil economy which we adopted last year, and when I came to the cold lunch and fried breakfast poor Evans' face fell; he evidently doesn't much believe in the virtue of food unless it is in the form of a 'hoosh' and has some chance of sticking to one's ribs. Lashly is to do all the cooking until we come to happier times, as he is far the best hand at the Primus, and can be relied upon not to exceed allowance."

After three days of this Scott was writing: "Lately we have been pulling for ten hours a day; it is rather too much when the strain on the harness is so great, and we are becoming gaunt shadows of ourselves. My companions' cheeks are quite sunken and hollow, and with their stubbly untrimmed beards and numerous frostbite remains they have the wildest appearance; yet we are all fit, and there has not been a sign of sickness beyond the return of those well remembered pangs of hunger which are now becoming exceedingly acute. We have at last finished our tobacco; for a long time Evans and I have had to be content with a half pipe a day, but now even that small comfort has gone, it was our long stay in the blizzard camp that has reduced us to this strait.''

13.12.03 We are still in the fog and bad weather. Had to camp early as we found we were going down hill and of course we did not know where.

When they started on 14th December visibility was bad and Scott had not "any notion" where they were. They were in danger of walking straight over a precipice, so they stopped for a council of war. The only result was to show more clearly that they were lost. Scott asked the men if they were prepared to go on in the circumstances. "They answered promptly in the affirmative. I think after our trying experiences we were all feeling pretty reckless." In any case, caution and undue delay meant eking out the slender rations still further.

They started down the slope with Scott in front to guide the sledge and Lashly and Evans behind to steady it and hold it back. As the slope increased footholds became less secure until in Scott's words: "Suddenly Lashly slipped, and in an instant he was sliding downward on his back; directly the strain came on Evans he too was thrown off his feet. It all happened in a moment, and before I had time to look the sledge and the two men hurtled past me; I braced myself to stop them, but might as well have attempted to hold an express train. With the first jerk I was whipped off my legs, and we all three lay sprawling on our backs and flying downward with ever increasing velocity. For some reason the first thought that flashed into my mind was that someone would break a limb if he attempted to stop our mad career, and I shouted something to this effect, but might as well have saved my breath. Then there came a sort of vague wonder as to what would happen next, and in the midst of this I was conscious that we had ceased to slide smoothly and were now bouncing over a rougher incline, sometimes leaving it for several yards at a time; my thoughts flew to broken limbs again, for I felt we could not stand much of such bumping. At length we gave a huge leap into the air, and yet we travelled with such velocity that I had no time to think before we came down with tremendous force on a gradual incline of rough, hard, wind-swept snow. Its irregularities brought us to rest in a moment or two, and I staggered to my feet in a dazed fashion, wondering what had happened. Then to my joy I saw the others also struggling to their legs, and in another moment I could thank heaven that no limbs were broken. But we had by no means escaped scatheless; our legs now showed one black bruise from knee to thigh, and Lashly was unfortunate enough to land once on his back, which is bruised and very painful. At the time, as can be imagined, we were all much shaken. I, as the lightest, escaped the easiest, yet before the two men crawled painfully to their feet their first question was to ask if I had been hurt."

Lashly had to make a much longer entry than usual to cover the events of this day.

14.12.03 It cleared a bit and we found we were on top of a cascade, and not a very nice looking one, so we commenced the descent and all went well till we were halfway down. Then the old sledge took charge and hauled the three of us down much faster than we wanted to go. But finally it brought up on some soft snow and capsized. When we could all speak we asked if anyone was hurt, but we all escaped with a few bruises luckily. We then gathered up our things and proceeded on our way. . .

Scott filled in the details: "As soon as I could pull myself together I looked round, and now to my astonishment I saw that we were well on toward the entrance of our own glacier; ahead and on either side of us appeared well-remembered landmarks, whilst behind, in the rough broken ice wall over which we had fallen, I now recognized at once the most elevated ice cascade of our valley. In the rude fashion which I have described we must have descended some 300 feet; above us the snowdrift was still being driven along, but the wind had not yet reached our present level, so that all around us the sky was bright and clear and our eyes could roam from one familiar object to another until far away to the Eastward they rested on the smoke capped summit of Erebus." It was a miraculous deliverance which left them within easy reach of their depot and plenty. They had a good lunch and set off to cover the last five or six miles to the depot.

Back in their usual places on the sledge, Scott in the middle and slightly in front, Lashly to his right, and Evans on the left, they went on. Lashly's entry for the 14th continued: "We came to the next cascade which was not so slippery, but very dangerous as it was full of crevasses. But we got over this without any accident. We had now descended about 2,000 feet, and was going along nicely . . ."

After a while the sledge began to skid and Scott told Lashly to pull wide to his right to steady it. No sooner had he moved out, when, as he went on:

The *Terra Nova* in a gale (*Paul Popper Ltd*)

Left: Chief Stoker William Lashly

Below: Inflating meteorological balloons (*Scott Polar Research Inst.*)

"All of a sudden the Captain and Evans disappeared down a crevasse and carried away one of the sledge runners, leaving me on top. It was now my duty to try and get them up again. After I saw they were safely dangling down there in space I at once secured the sledge with a pair of ski, and held on to the other end while the Captain climbed up out. Rather a difficult thing to do especially as his hands were getting frost-bitten all the time. But finally he succeeded. We then pulled Evans up and once more proceeded on our way down to the Nunotak where we camped in the calm and warmest corner we had found for the last five weeks, and pretty well in safety."

Scott gave a fuller account: "By a miracle Lashly saved himself from following, and sprang back with his whole weight on the trace; the sledge flashed by him and jumped the crevasse down which we had gone, one side of its frame cracked through in the jerk which followed, but the other side mercifully held. Personally I remember absolutely nothing until I found myself dangling at the end of my trace with blue walls on either side and a very horrid looking gulf below; large ice-crystals dislodged by our movements continued to shower down on our heads. As a first step I took off my goggles; I then discovered that Evans was hanging just above me. I asked him if he was all right, and received a reassuring reply in his usual calm, matter of fact tones. Meanwhile I groped about on every side with my cramponed feet, only to find everywhere the same slippery smooth wall. But my struggles had set me swinging, and at one end of a swing my leg suddenly struck a projection. In a moment I had turned, and saw at a glance that by raising myself I could get a foothold on it; with the next swing I clutched it with my steel-shod feet, and after a short struggle succeeded in partly transferring my weight to it. In this position, with my feet firmly planted and my balance maintained by my harness, I could look about me. I found myself standing on a thin shaft of ice which was wedged between the walls of the chasm—how it came to be there I cannot imagine, but its position was wholly providential; to the right or left, above or below, there was not the vestige of another such support—nothing in fact, but the smooth walls of ice. My next step was to get Evans into the same position as myself, and when he had slipped his harness well up under his arms I found I could pilot his feet to the bridge.

"All this had occupied some time and it was only now that I realized what had happened above us, for there, some twelve feet over our heads, was the outline of the broken sledge. I saw at once what a frail support remained, and shouted to Lashly to ask what he could do, and then I knew the value of such a level headed companion; for whilst he held on grimly to the sledge and us with one hand, his other was busily employed in withdrawing our ski. At length he succeeded in sliding two of these beneath the broken sledge and so making our support more secure. The device was well thought of, but it still left us without his active assistance; for, as he told us, directly he relaxed his strain the sledge began to slip, and he dare not trust only to the ski."

When Scott climbed out and flung himself panting and frozen on top Lashly said, "Thank God." "It was perhaps then," Scott said, "that I realized that his position had been the worst of all." With Evans safely up he said: "For a minute or two we could only look at one another, then Evans said, 'Well I'm blowed,' it was the first sign of astonishment he had shown."

Scott described the scene at camp that night: "We dawdled over everything. We were sore and weary, yet Lashly sang a merry stave as he stirred the pot, and Evans and I sat on the sledge, shifted our footgear, spread our garments out to dry, and chatted away merrily the whole time. Evans' astonishment at the events of the day seemed to grow ever deeper, and was exhibited in the most amusing manner. With his sock half on he would pause and think out our adventures in some new light and would say suddenly, 'Well, sir, but what about that snow bridge?' or, if so and so hadn't happened 'where should we be now', and then the soliloquy would end with 'my word, but it was a close call!' Evans generally manages to sum a case up fairly pithily, and perhaps this last remark is a comprehensive description of our experiences."

On the next day Scott wrote: "We all agree that yesterday was the most adventurous day of our lives, and we none of us want to have another like it."

15.12.03 This was a beautiful morning. I had to put the German silver on our runners, so we did not get on the way before 12 o'clock. When we started we had another nine foot sledge to pull. It was left here last year. We got down the glacier about 16 miles and camped for the night. Tomorrow we hope to reach "B" depot and have a good feed. I have got a touch of snow-blindness.

And that was the last entry in Lashly's *Discovery* diary.

Although they were almost within sight of the ship they had not quite finished. Scott was determined to explore one of the tributaries of the glacier. He led off down a steep ice slope which they had to negotiate roped together. There were streams of running thaw water and a frozen lake resting on a deep moraine of mud. Lashly thought it was "a splendid place for growing spuds". They came to a long stretch of undulating sand with shallow ice-free lakes. Scott went on: "I was so fascinated by all these strange new sights that I strode forward without thought of hunger until Evans asked if it was any use carrying our lunch further; we all decided that it wasn't and so sat down on a small hillock of sand with a merry little stream gurgling over the pebbles at our feet. It was a very cheery meal, and certainly the most extraordinary we have had. We commanded an extensive view both up and down the valley, and yet, except about the rugged mountain summits, there was not a vestige of ice or snow to be seen; and as we ran the comparatively warm sand through our fingers and quenched our thirst at the stream, it seemed almost impossible that we could be within a hundred miles of the terrible conditions we had experienced on the summit. It was nearly four o'clock before we turned towards our camp, and nearly ten before we reached it, feeling that it was quite time for supper. The day's record, however, is a pretty good tribute to our marching power, for we have walked and climbed over the roughest country, for more than fourteen hours with only one brief halt for lunch.''

CHAPTER 9

FREED FROM THE ICE

THEY GOT BACK to the *Discovery* on Christmas Eve, 1903. Christmas Day—Lashly's 36th birthday—was spent in comfort on board.

Reporting on the Western Journey Scott said: "I am bound to confess that I have some pride in this journey. We met with immense difficulties, such as would have brought us hopelessly to grief in the previous year, yet now as veterans we steered through them with success; and when all circumstances are considered, the extreme severity of the climate and the obstacles that stood in our path, I cannot but believe we came near the limit of possible performance. We may claim, therefore, to have accomplished a creditable journey under the hardest conditions on record."

In the journeys they had made together this season Scott, Lashly, and Evans had covered 1,098 miles at an average of 15·4 miles a day. Scott noted some odd effects after a few days on board with unaccustomed quantities of food and sleep: "Lashly was a man who usually changed little, and therefore he quickly fell back into his ordinary condition, but Evans continued to expand, and reached quite an alarming maximum before he slowly returned to his normal size."

During their absence, the ship had been prepared for sea, and the sawing camp had been established some 10½ miles from the ship; there was still no sign of the ice breaking up. Scott's restless energy, and the urgent necessity to get away from the temptation of too much food, drove him on. On 31st December:

"We three packed our sledge once more and started away."
This same tone of content and comradeship with his men was
apparent when they reached the sawing camp: "It is a real treat
to be amongst our people once more and to find them in such
splendid condition and spirits. I do not think there is a whole
garment in the party; judging by the torn and patched clothing,
they might be the veriest lot of tramps, but one would have to
go far to find such sturdy tramps. Everyone is burnt to a deep
bronze colour by the sun, but in each dark face one has not to
wait long for the smiles which show the white of teeth and clear
healthy eyes."

The camp was halfway to the ice edge—as close as they
dared go for fear of it breaking away unexpectedly. So there
were twenty miles of ice to saw through. It was a hopeless task
in ice that was between six and seven feet thick. After 12 days
they had cut a channel 150 yards long. In spite of this Scott was
able to report: "I do not think I ever saw such exuberant, over-
flowing health and spirits as now exist in this camp. It is a good
advertisement for teetotallers, as there is no grog, and our
strongest drinks are tea and cocoa, but of course the most potent
factor is the outdoor life with the hard work and good food.
Apart from the work, everyone agrees that it has been the most
splendid picnic they have ever had."

Two ships were sighted on 5th January, 1904. As well as the
Morning there was a second relief ship—the *Terra Nova*. The
reports sent home in the *Morning* the year before had alarmed
the authorities at home and galvanized them into action. If the
Discovery could not be freed this year she was to be abandoned.
Relief of the crew, possibly on account of the mention of scurvy,
was considered essential. Although, as Scott said: "We considered ourselves well able to cope with any situation that might
arise, and believed that we were quite capable of looking after
ourselves." So the *Terra Nova* had been chartered, fitted out,

and provisioned with all haste. She was even towed through the Mediterranean by relays of cruisers to save time sailing her round the Cape of Good Hope. "Cruiser after cruiser took her in tow and raced her through the water at a speed which must have surprised the barnacles on her stout wooden sides."

On 15th January they started to transport stores, instruments, specimens and valuables across the ice to the relief ships. Every day the semaphore station on Tent Island reported by special code of flags and shapes: "No change in the ice." By 1st February the ice edge had started to break up and the relief ships were getting closer—"an even chance" Scott called it. Blasting the ice with dynamite made no impression. The 150 yard channel they had sawn broke away in the middle of a flow without even helping to crack it into smaller pieces. By 14th February, when it looked as though the *Discovery* would not be freed in time, a dramatic change took place. By some huge unseen force, the ice began to break up, and stream away out to sea. The relief ships approached until the *Terra Nova* could pass a line to the *Discovery*. The last piece of ice, 12 feet thick, that still held her was broken up by blasting, and, on 16th February, she was free again. But the very next day a fierce gale sprang up and, while trying to make for open water, the *Discovery* was driven inshore and grounded. She was aground from 11 a.m. to 8 p.m. pounding on a shoal until all on board thought she must be wrecked. Her stout build proved equal to the battering she received until at last she slid off into deeper water and was safely afloat again.

Scott wanted to explore the coastline to the north-west before sailing for good and the *Discovery* needed coal. On 18th February the weather had moderated and they went to work, taking in coal first from the *Terra Nova* and then from the *Morning*. Coaling was always hard work, and coming on top of the rigours of the last 24 hours it was particularly arduous. "Now,

as always," wrote Scott, "the manner in which our people under-
took a heavy task and worked on at it without rest was a sight
for the gods. Perhaps the strongest support of this splendid
spirit was the fact that on such occasions, by mutual consent,
there was no distinction between officers and men." Scott's final
report to the Admiralty included more on this theme: "On
polar expeditions there must always be times when all must
work for the common good, regardless of department; at such
times there has been no need to ask for volunteers in the
Discovery. On the sledges, or on the snow, in coaling or working
the ship, or at any task that needed to be done hurriedly,
officers and men have worked alike, and grudged no labour
until the work was finished. The conduct of the men has been
beyond praise. By them the monotony of the second winter was
met with unfailing cheerfulness. Most arduous sledge journeys
and the most severe weather were encountered in the same
spirit and with an intelligence that freed the officers from all
anxiety as to their welfare. But the qualities of the ship's
company have never been more evident than since our release
from the ice. The difficulties which might be expected after such
a long captivity in the ice were overcome only by incessant
labour. It was, in the sailor's expression, 'Watch on, Stop on,'
and though many were almost worn out with fatigue, there was
neither complaint nor demur when a fresh task was imposed.
I shall hope to make their services better known to you on the
return of the expedition."

Fate had one last throw in store for them. It was rough on
22nd February and the pumps stopped working. The water
rose to the stokehold plates and fires had to be drawn so the
steam pump stopped. The hand pumps were out of action so
all the pumps were stripped down but were found to be in
working order. Then they examined the pump suctions. These
were found to be choked solid with ash and when they had been

cleared the hand pumps got the water down enough for fires to be relit and steam pumps started. The trouble was caused by the fact that the bilges were solid with ice on sailing. It had been thought that the ice would melt when the ship was steaming and the water be pumped out. No one had reckoned with the ashes in the bilge ice blocking the pump suctions. The Engine Room staff worked for 24 hours without a spell to put the trouble right. For Lashly it was an experience that was to be repeated six years later with more serious results.

On 5th March, 1904, the *Discovery*'s head was finally turned for home. A month later, on Good Friday, she led the *Terra Nova* and *Morning* into Lyttelton Harbour in New Zealand. She sailed again on 8th June and steered for Cape Horn to complete the magnetic survey part of the programme. Adverse winds forced them to make the passage through the Magellan Straits, reaching Port Stanley in the Falkland Islands on 12th July. There they took in coal for the long trip home and reached Spithead on 10th September, 1904, three years and one month after sailing. The *Discovery* paid off at the end of the month and there were two months' leave for each man.

Scott's task now was to make a full report to the Admiralty, and, first of all, he asked for "some substantial reward for the men." He went on: "It is to be observed, and the men are fully aware, that they have lost much by their long absence from the regular service. The men are prepared to do their utmost to regain the lost ground, but I would submit that My Lords should be pleased to direct that they should have every facility which is conformable with the efficiency of the service in qualifying for such gunnery or torpedo ratings as they may wish to obtain." Lashly was promoted to Chief Stoker immediately for his services on the expedition, and the promotion was back-dated to 1st June, 1902. Evans was promoted Petty Officer

1st Class, back-dated to April, 1904, and he went to the gunnery school at Portsmouth to qualify. Crean was recommended for promotion to Petty Officer 1st Class, and his promotion dated from the day the *Discovery* got home, he served in all the ships commanded by Scott afterwards always in the capacity of Captain's Coxwain. All the members of the expedition received the Antarctic Medal.

Scott's report went on: "I feel that it is most difficult to place before My Lords in its true light the exemplary behaviour of the officers and men lent to the expedition. It is to be remembered that they were not under the Naval Discipline Act, and were perfectly well aware of the feeble application of the Merchant Shipping Laws to their unusual position. If it was by my suggestion, it was by their choice, that the true spirit of naval discipline was observed throughout the voyage and I cannot remember a single incidence of a man presuming on the laxity of the law, or acting otherwise than he would had he been on the decks of a man-of-war. The same relations were observed between officers and men as are customary in H.M. ships and the same practical obedience to command was invariably given, with perhaps an unusual intelligence in obeying the spirit rather than the letter of the order. I would protest emphatically that this was not done with the hope of reward, because from the first I pointed out that under the exceptional conditions, a reward was improbable. I sincerely believe that the excellent conduct was due to a high sense of duty and that they worked purely for the honour of their ship, their service and their country.

"Both in New Zealand and at home they have been feted, and made much of, and fully exposed to all the temptations which so frequently demoralize men of their class. It must be considered no small addition to their credit that they have come through such an ordeal unscathed and have preserved their good name to the end. Where a whole ship's company has acted with such extraordinary zeal and loyalty, it is difficult and almost invidious to mention particular services. I have therefore in the accompanying remarks mentioned only such cases as may appear exceptional in the rewards suggested.

"The Officers will be the last to forget how much they owe to the rank and file."

Lashly and Evans came in for special mention: "These are both men of magnificent physique. They accompanied me on my sledge journey to the interior of Victoria Land. I would remark that I think that journey nearly reached the limit of performance possible under the conditions, in order to point out that it could not have been accomplished had either of these men failed in the smallest degree. Their determination, courage, and patience were often taxed to the utmost, yet I never knew them other than cheerful and respectful. On one occasion Lashly undoubtedly saved our lives by his presence of mind when Evans and I had fallen into a crevasse."

CHAPTER 10

INTERLUDE

AFTER HIS RETURN Lashly slipped unobtrusively into the ordinary naval life of a Chief Stoker. It came as no surprise to those who knew him that he was sent to the Royal Naval College at Osborne as an instructor to the Officer Cadets.

His shipmates remembered him, in their own words, as modest, reserved, hardworking, helpful, skilful, completely dependable, and a friend of all. One of them summed him up quite simply as the salt of the earth.

The officers and men of the Last Expedition knew something of Lashly's qualities in advance, as they knew something of Dr Bill Wilson's qualities. Nature had endowed both these men with a full share of human virtues. Of Wilson, the fast friend and confidant of all the officers, Scott said: "The finest character I ever met." Of Lashly the officers said: "The Wilson of the lower deck." They said, too, that if Scott had taken Lashly to the Pole things most surely would have turned out differently.

Six years after the *Discovery's* return, steaming down McMurdo Sound in the *Terra Nova*, Lashly was standing on deck talking to another man. He pointed out the Dry Valley down which he had walked with Scott after the crevasse fall. "Excuse me," said Frank Debenham, who was standing just behind them and could not help overhearing, "that's not the Dry Valley, it's the next one." "Ah! sir," said Lashly, "you must be one of Shackleton's men, and I dare say you are right." Debenham admitted that he was a new boy but said he knew

the *Voyage of the Discovery* and all the maps backwards. They
introduced themselves, and Debenham was covered in confusion.
A few miles on Lashly could see he had been mistaken, and he
was amused to think he had not been able to recognize where
he had been.

PART II

THE LAST EXPEDITION

Shore Parties

Robert Falcon Scott	Captain, C.V.O., R.N.
Edward R. G. R. Evans	Lieutenant, R.N.
Victor L. A. Campbell	Lieutenant, R.N. (Emergency List)
Henry R. Bowers	Lieutenant, R.I.M.
Lawrence E. G. Oates	Captain 6th Inniskilling Dragoons
G. Murray Levick	Surgeon, R.N.
Edward L. Atkinson	Surgeon, R.N., Parasitologist

Scientific Staff

Edward Adrian Wilson	B.A., M.B. (Cantab.), Chief of the Scientific Staff, and Zoologist
George C. Simpson	D.Sc., Meteorologist
T. Griffith Taylor	B.A., B.Sc., B.E., Geologist
Edward W. Belson	Biologist
Frank Debenham	B.A., B.Sc., Geologist
Charles S. Wright	B.A., Physicist
Raymond E. Priestley	Geologist
Herbert G. Ponting	F.R.G.S., Camera Artist
Cecil H. Meares	In charge of dogs
Bernard C. Day	Motor Engineer
Apsley Cherry-Garrard	B.A., Assistant Zoologist
Tryggve Gran	Sub-Lieutenant, Norwegian N.R., B.A., Ski Expert

Men

W. Lashly	Chief Stoker, R.N.
W. W. Archer	Chief Steward, Late R.N. (second winter only)
Thomas Clissold	Cook, Late R.N.
Edgar Evans	Petty Officer, R.N.
Robert Forde	Petty Officer, R.N.
Thomas Crean	Petty Officer, R.N.
Thomas S. Williamson	Petty Officer, R.N. (second winter only)
Patrick Keohane	Petty Officer, R.N.
George P. Abbott	Petty Officer, R.N.
Frank V. Browning	Petty Officer, 2nd Class, R.N.

Harry Dickason	Able Seaman, R.N.
F. J. Hooper	Steward, Late R.N.
Anton Omelchenko	Groom
Demetri Gerof	Dog Driver

CHAPTER 11

THE LAST EXPEDITION

LASHLY, EDGAR EVANS and Tom Crean were natural choices, out of nearly 8,000 volunteers, for Scott's last Expedition. They joined the *Terra Nova* in the spring of 1910. She was 25 years old by then but there was no other ship available as the *Discovery* had been chartered by the Hudson's Bay Company. The expedition sailed from Cardiff on 15th June, 1910, and went by way of Madeira, Simonstown and Melbourne, to Lyttelton once more. It was at Melbourne that Scott received the telegram from Amundsen which read: "Madeira; am going South." The news was like a bolt from the blue. Up to that time it was generally believed that Amundsen was fitting out the *Fram* for further Arctic exploration. Scott's plan to reach the South Pole had been widely publicized in his fund raising campaign.

Final preparations were hastened along at Lyttelton. All the stores had to be landed, sorted and restowed. Mrs Scott was frequently to be seen sitting on a crate on the dockside, list in hand, checking over the stores. The hut was erected ashore to make certain there would be no snags or delays in building it in the Antarctic because this time they were to live in it. The ship was docked to make good defects found on the voyage out, decks were caulked, and leaks below the water line were stopped with cement. Stalls were built under the forecastle, and on deck, for the 19 ponies that were to be embarked, and soon everything was ready.

The ship sailed from Dunedin for the Antarctic on 29th

November, 1910, looking, as Lieutenant Evans, the second-in-command, described it, like a floating farmyard. The ponies, their forage, 34 sledge dogs and a few pet rabbits were all on the upper deck. Thirty tons of coal in sacks, two and a half tons of petrol, paraffin, and three huge crates containing the motor sledges made up the deck cargo: "Not an inch of deck space was visible." The men had asked through Petty Officer Evans that their comfort should not be considered, and they gave up a good deal of their messdeck space to allow all the stores to be squeezed on board. The ship was badly overloaded for her journey across the world's stormiest seas, but there was no alternative. She was registered as a yacht because Captain Scott had been elected a member of the Royal Yacht Squadron and so the normal loading rules did not apply. Lieutenant Evans said he painted out the Plimsoll mark and it was nearly one foot under water, but Scott said it was still three inches above the water line.

The wind got up the first day out, and by 1st December it was blowing a full gale. On 2nd December the wind was logged as force 10. Mountainous seas swept right over the decks and the deck cargo started to break adrift. Coal sacks acted as battering rams and threatened to break the drums of petrol and paraffin adrift. They tried oil to stop the seas breaking, but in the end they had to throw ten tons of coal overboard. The dogs were in danger of being strangled on their leashes and the ponies were badly knocked about. Worst of all the deck seams opened with the violent movement of the ship and water poured below, washing quantities of coal dust into the bilges. This combined with oil, always present in ships' bilges, to form hard balls which choked the pump suctions.

Scott wrote in his diary: "From 4 a.m. the Engine Room became the centre of interest. The water gained in spite of every effort. Lashly, to his neck in rushing water, stuck gamely to the work of clearing suctions."

In spite of Lashly's efforts, the stokehold plates were soon under water. The ash pit filled, and there was danger of the water coming in contact with the boiler plates. If this had been allowed to happen the boiler would have buckled and been useless for further steaming. The fires had to be drawn and the ship was at the mercy of the storm. The main steam pump stopped, and the hand pump suctions were choked with the pellets of coal dust and oil. As a last resort a chain gang of officers, scientists, and men started to bale the ship out with buckets.

This just about kept the water level from rising any more, but they had to get at the source of the trouble. In sweltering heat, the engineers got behind the boiler and cut a hole in the bulkhead so that Lieutenant Evans and Lieutenant Bowers could crawl through and climb down to the hand pump suction well. They managed to reach out the oily lumps of coal that were blocking it, often submerging completely in the filthy oily water. At last, the hand pump was working again and began to gain on the water below. The weather moderated next day, fires were relit, and the ship was pumped dry. It had been a close call, and three ponies and a dog had died in the chaos on deck. Osman, the lead dog, had been washed overboard as well, but, luckily, the next wave swept him back again.

Icebergs were sighted on 7th December, and on the 9th they were in the pack ice. The pack that year was encountered further north than on any previous expedition, and it extended for about 400 miles. It was the biggest field of ice on record. Progress was desperately slow. Sometimes the ship was stopped altogether and fires were let out to economize in coal. When the floes were not too thick the ship was steamed at them to open up a lead by butting her way through.

The *Terra Nova*, in her day, had been one of the finest Scottish whalers afloat and was well equipped for this sort of struggle. Built of oak, her sides were 14 inches thick with an iron shod stem which was nine feet thick. Even so, she did not get clear of the pack ice until 29th December, which was much later than Scott had hoped. This delay and the loss of three ponies did not augur well for the future.

Scott wanted to make his winter quarters at Cape Crozier which was the spot chosen by Dr Wilson as being the best for the continuity of the scientific work started on the *Discovery* expedition. It was a place familiar to Lashly who had been there just over eight years before when Lieutenant Skelton was the first man to set eyes on the Emperor Penguin rookery. But the swell under the cliffs there made a landing impossible, and the ship steamed round into McMurdo Sound. The sea ice was still in and there was no hope of reaching Hut Point and the old *Discovery* hut, so the *Terra Nova* was secured alongside the ice edge about a mile and a half from a little promontory that was christened Cape Evans. This was to be winter quarters, and the work of unloading began straight away.

It was 4th January, 1911, later than planned because of the delay in the pack ice, and it was vitally important to get the base set up and working without further loss of time. Hut Point and the barrier were 15 miles away and the journey had to be made over the sea ice, because the land route was too rough to be passable with ponies. The depot laying journey had to start as soon as possible to take advantage of what was left of the Antarctic summer, and before the ice broke up and went out to sea. It was light round the clock at this time and they worked long hours. The dogs and ponies were soon hard at it running loads ashore, stretching their legs, and starting to get fit after the long confinement on board.

Two of the motor sledges were landed the first day and were soon in action towing loaded sledges to the shore. Bernard Day, who was in charge of the motor transport, had had previous experience with a motor car on Shackleton's expedition. He and Captain Scott had taken one of the motor sledges to Norway for trials before the expedition sailed. Subsequently, Lashly, as one of the drivers, had been for a short course at the Wolseley Tool and Motor Company's works at Birmingham. The man who showed him the motors there found him "most eager and alert for knowledge".

The motor sledges were very advanced machines for the time, forerunners of the tanks of World War I. They had special four-cylinder air-cooled Wolseley engines of 12 horse power, which gave a top speed of $3\frac{1}{2}$ miles per hour. There were two forward gears, no reverse, no steering and no brakes. Steering was effected by a steersman harnessed to a pole in front on which he pulled as required. There was magneto ignition and a special carburettor heating device. To keep down the weight the chassis and frame members were made of ash, and the pads of the tracks were of plywood fitted with spikes.

In spite of the fact that rough seas had washed over the crates continuously in the great gale Scott said the motors came out of their boxes looking "as fresh and clean as if they had been packed on the previous day". Over a good surface they could pull a ton, and the timbers for the hut were in the first loads.

"The motor sledges are working well, but not very well," wrote Scott. "The small difficulties will be got over, but I rather fear they will never draw the loads we expect of them. Still, they promise to be a help, and they are a lively and attractive feature of our present scene as they drone along over the floe. At a little distance, without silencers, they sound exactly like threshing machines." The motors proved most useful for hauling empty sledges out to the ship again. The man-haulers took full advantage of this but the motors never did well enough for Scott to place any reliance on them in his plans for the polar march. "Day," he wrote later, "is quite convinced he will go a long way and is prepared to accept much heavier weights than I have given him. Lashly's opinion is perhaps more doubtful, but on the whole hopeful." Lashly's naval training had made him more of a blacksmith than a mechanic, but he had mastered the mechanics of the motor sledges. Tryggve Gran said: "Whatever he did was first class. Day could not have had a more all-round helper."

The third motor sledge was hoisted out on 8th January. This one had been fitted with a winch as a useful extra, but its usefulness was never put to the test. A thaw had set in and the ice near the ship was getting very soft and was beginning to break away altogether. The motor was moved to firmer ice but even so it began to sink in. They put a tow line on it and all available men tried to pull it to safety. Again the sledge started to sink through and its weight began to pull the men back. Each was forced to let go as he was dragged to the lip of the hole and eventually the sledge sank and was lost for good.

The depot laying party got away on 24th January and the very next day all the sea ice in the bays broke up and disappeared out to sea, closing the route from Cape Evans to Hut Point and the barrier behind them. Lashly did not go on this trip. He was an experienced sledger anyway, and his handy-man abilities were needed to get the base working properly. The stables had to be completed and there were nine ponies left behind to be taken care of. Lashly was an automatic choice for this job, and he helped the Russian groom Anton.

CHAPTER 12

PREPARATIONS FOR
THE SOUTHERN ADVANCE

THE TWO DEPOTS to be stocked on the depot laying journey were Corner Camp and One Ton Depot. Corner Camp was the spot where the barrier route turned south after passing the crevassed pressure area in the vicinity of White Island. It was about 35 miles from Hut Point. One Ton Depot was to be the last depot laid in advance of the polar journey. Scott wanted to put it at 80° South, about 170 miles from Hut Point.

A blizzard at Corner Camp held up the depot laying party for three whole days. It left a soft surface for marching on, so that the ponies, whose condition deteriorated rapidly in the blizzard, often sank to their bellies in the snow. Scott was forced to modify his plan and lay One Ton Depot at 79° 30° South—30 miles further north than he intended. Five ponies were lost on the return march. Two died of exhaustion, and three had to be killed before they were taken by killer whales when the sea ice, on which they were crossing from the barrier to the Hut Point Peninsula, broke up while they were on it.

The dog teams, on the other hand, were very successful on this journey. So much so that Scott mentioned to Lieutenant Evans the possibility of running them light on the barrier stage of the polar journey, and then using them for hauling on the polar plateau stage.

The ship in the meantime had steamed east along the barrier to land a party under Lieutenant Campbell to explore King Edward VII land. When they got to the Bay of Whales, Scott's

Balloon Bight, they were amazed to see a ship secured alongside the barrier. It was the *Fram*, and Amundsen and his Norwegians were setting up camp a couple of miles inland on the barrier. Amundsen said afterwards that from his study of previous expeditions he had no doubt that the Bay of Whales was a permanent feature of the barrier face and that the barrier was aground at this point. He had made straight for it and was confident that there was no danger of his camp site breaking away. Johanssen, the man who had accompanied Nansen on his great North Polar trek, was a member of the *Fram*'s crew, but he did not accompany Amundsen to the Pole.

Amundsen had no less than 116 dogs with him—he had not lost a single one on the trip from Norway. Indeed, the ten bitches amongst them had reared puppies successfully. Campbell's party could not land there too, so, after exchanging greetings with the Norwegians, the *Terra Nova* hurried back to Hut Point to leave a note with this momentous news which Scott would get on his return from the depot journey. Then Campbell and his men were landed at Cape Adare in which neighbourhood they were to remain, in conditions of appalling hardship, for the next eighteen months.

While these events were taking place other parties were active at Cape Evans and in the Western Mountains where a four-man party led by Griffith Taylor had started on a geological survey. Petty Officer Evans had gone with this party as the experienced sledge hand to show the others the ropes. After helping Anton complete the fittings and furnishings of the stables, Lashly went with a small party under Ponting to Shackleton's old hut at Cape Royds. Day, the engineer, went as well to see the hut that had been his home for so long on that expedition. The inside of the hut was exactly as it had been left after the hurried departure of that expedition. Outside they saw

the body of one of Shackleton's ponies floating in the appro-
priately named Dead Horse Bay. Oddly enough it was washed
away the very next day when Ponting and Lashly were catching
an octopus in the bay.

Scott got back to Hut Point on 22nd February to learn the
news about Amundsen. The sea ice was still out and the party
could not return to Cape Evans. There was plenty of time for
Scott to reflect on the new situation, and his thoughts were set
down in his diary.

"One thing only fixes itself definitely in my mind," he wrote.
"The proper, as well as the wiser, course for us is to proceed
exactly as though this had not happened. To go forward, to do
our best for the honour of our country without fear or panic.
There is no doubt that Amundsen's plan is a very serious
menace to ours. He has a shorter distance to the pole by 60
miles—I never thought he could have got so many dogs safely
to the ice. His plan for running them seems excellent. But above
and beyond all he can start his journey earlier in the season—
an impossible condition with ponies."

The setbacks to Scott's plans were formidable. The delay in
the pack ice caused the depot journey to start late, which, with
the blizzard at Corner Camp, resulted in One Ton Depot being
left thirty miles too far north. And there were only ten ponies
left—five lost on the depot journey, three lost in the great gale
at sea, and one had died at Cape Evans. In Scott's favour was
the fact that Amundsen would have to travel an unexplored
route. The barrier stage would probably be straightforward,
but he would have to be lucky to find a route up the coastal
mountains to the polar plateau. Scott was going to use the route
previously explored by Shackleton up the Beardmore glacier.
This huge valley glacier, which stretched for more than 120 miles
from the sea level barrier surface to the polar plateau 10,000

feet above, was known to be passable. It varied in width from 10 to 30 miles wide.

It is clear from his diary that Scott never intended to make a race of it. He even revised his ideas about the use of his dogs, and said later that he was disappointed with their performance to date. It seems probable that he recalled his unfortunate experience with dogs in the *Discovery* days. He made up his mind to rely on ponies to pull to the foot of the Beardmore where they would have to be killed, while the dog teams returned to Hut Point. Scott had less compunction about killing ponies for dog food, and human food, and this formed part of his plan. Amundsen was quite ruthless in his use of dogs and had no hesitation in killing them off as the loads diminished. The carcasses were fed to the other dogs and he and his men ate dog meat. He told Lieutenant Evans afterwards: "If I wanted fresh meat I killed a dog." At the end of his journey he only had 11 left out of the 52 that set out.

Scott had to stay at Hut Point until the middle of April. The Western Geological party had arrived there too and with the two surviving ponies to be sheltered as well, the old *Discovery* hut really came into its own. There was a gale in March during which the outer two miles of the Glacier Tongue broke off and floated away. For one moment Scott had considered building the hut on it but this incident demonstrated very clearly the dangers of placing any reliance on the permanence of barrier ice formation, except where it was known to be aground.

On 12th April the sea ice at Cape Evans was just nine inches thick when Lashly dashed into the hut to report that there was a large party coming round the Cape. This was Scott with some of the men from Hut Point after a perilous journey partly by the land route and partly on sea ice that was not really safe. On

17th April he was off again with a party of fresh men to relieve those still at Hut Point. Lashly went with him this time to look after the two ponies still left at Hut Point, with strict instructions not to attempt to return to Cape Evans until the journey could be made safely on sea ice all the way. This was Lashly's first trip with Scott since *Discovery* days: "Lashly splendid at camp work as of old . . . I am greatly struck with the advantages of experience in Crean and Lashly for all work about camp."

It was not until 13th May that the party could return to Cape Evans. The two ponies were in good health, and the men, black with soot from the blubber stove, were cheerful and fit.

CHAPTER 13

WINTER IN THE HUT AT CAPE EVANS

THE MIDDLE OF May, 1911, saw the whole party of 25 assembled in the Hut at Cape Evans for the winter. The hut was 50 feet long by 25 feet wide and was divided into wardroom and messdeck by a bulkhead of provision boxes, which became cupboards as they were emptied. The sixteen officers and scientists, the two laboratories, and the dark-room occupied two-thirds of the hut. The other third was messdeck and galley, with a galley stove that kept the whole hut warm. The bunks were the ordinary wire mattress type arranged singly or in tiers as space demanded. Lashly's sleeping billet was an individual contraption slung by rods from the roof over the ends of the bunks occupied by Clissold, the cook, and Hooper, the steward. The hut was double glazed and had two thicknesses of boarding with seaweed and rubberoid insulation between. It was lit by an acetylene plant housed in the porch between the double doors.

Clissold rigged up an ingenious alarm system to warn himself when the next batch of bread was ready for baking. A metal disc on top of the dough completed an electric circuit when it was sufficiently risen and rang a bell at his bunk. It alerted everyone besides the cook and when the novelty soon wore off he was forced to substitute a red lamp for the bell. It became the duty of the night watchman to shake him when the lamp burned. The task of night watchman was undertaken by the "afterguard"—the officers and scientists—and Captain Scott always took his turn with the others. It meant taking the

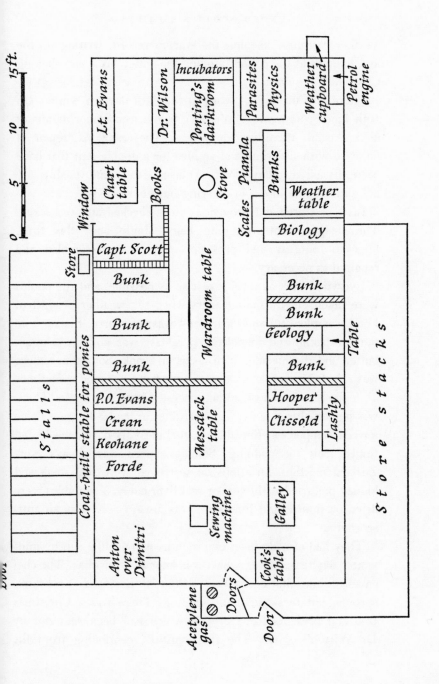

weather readings, keeping the Aurora record, writing up the log, looking at the ponies, stoking the galley fire—and shaking Clissold as required.

There was no lack of work in the dark days of winter. On 10th June Scott wrote: "We have begun to consider details of next season's travelling equipment. The crampons, repair of finnesko with seal skin, and an idea for a double tent that have been discussed today. Petty Officer Evans and Lashly are delightfully intelligent in carrying out instructions."

Lists of stores and provisions were checked and rechecked. The sledges, tents, sleeping bags, single ones this time, finnesko footgear and provision bags were assembled and repaired as necessary.

Everyone took as much exercise as possible, and the ponies were taken out by their leaders when the weather permitted. Food was plentiful and varied and was, of course, the same in the wardroom and messdeck. Breakfast was porridge, bread, butter and marmalade, with cocoa to drink. Sometimes there was fish if any had been caught in the fish traps, and sometimes Truegg. Lunch was bread and cheese with cocoa again. There was jam on alternate days, and sardines or lambs' tongues twice a week. Supper was tinned soup, seal meat six days a week, and tinned fruit for pudding. Sunday supper was always New Zealand mutton. Variations on seal meat were seal steak and kidney pie, fried seal liver, or seal liver curry. Vegetables were dried or tinned, and lime juice was always served as an anti-scorbutic.

They had already been two months without the sun by midwinter day, 22nd June, which was kept as Christmas. The chef excelled himself. There was sirloin of beef and Yorkshire, sprouts, potatoes and plum pudding. There was a Christmas tree and presents for everyone which had been sent out by Dr Wilson's sister. The third edition, continuing from the

Discovery days, of the *South Polar Times* appeared, reaching its customary high standard.

Church services were held every Sunday, with hymns played by Cherry-Garrard on the pianola. The singing was led by a choir composed of Scott, Wilson, Bowers, Debenham and Lashly. Lashly had always been a church-going man, and had even been a bell-ringer at the church at Hambledon.

The South Polar University was in session three nights a week for purely voluntary attendance. The experts lectured on their own subjects, and Ponting often gave magic lantern shows with slides made on his travels around the world. One evening Scott gave the long awaited talk on "Future Plans" for the Polar march. He estimated 144 days for the return journey— 82 days to the Pole, 53 days to return to One Ton Depot, and the rest back to base. It meant he would not get back till 27th March, 1912, which was too late to expect the ship to be still in the South. The main party would have to spend a second winter in the Antarctic. Their late return was the result of a late start due to using ponies. Dogs could travel on soft snow, but ponies, with their sharp hooves, would sink right through at each step.

On 27th June Dr Bill Wilson set out with his team for the Winter Journey to Cape Crozier to study the nesting habits of the Emperor Penguin. He had been nursing this project ever since Skelton and Petty Officer Evans had photographed the rookery there on Lashly's second sledge trip in October, 1902, and Royds had brought back the egg a month later. Lashly had noted at the time "they lay very early". No one had ever made a journey in the extreme cold and total darkness of an Antarctic mid-winter. Bowers and Cherry-Garrard went with him. "This winter travel is a new and bold venture, but the right men have gone to attempt it," wrote Scott. In *The Worst Journey* Cherry-Garrard said: "I don't know. There never could have been any doubt about Bill and Birdie. Probably Lashly would have made the best third, but Bill had a prejudice against seamen for a journey like this—'They don't take enough care of themselves, and they will not look after their clothes.' But Lashly was wonderful—if Scott had only taken a four-man party and Lashly to the Pole."

They were away 5 weeks and came back in a very run down condition, suffering from frostbite and the first symptoms of scurvy. "We slept a thousand thousand years," wrote Cherry-Garrard. The next afternoon, when he came to again, he found Lashly had already cut his hair.

Ponting, the expedition's camera artist, was naturally an acute observer of the daily scene. In his book *The Great White South* he mentioned the messdeck personalities. "In the mess-deck Petty Officer Evans was the dominant personality. His previous Polar experience, his splendid build, and his stentorian voice and manner of using it all compelled the respect due to one who would have been conspicuous in any company. He also, was one of the leader's towers of strength. More than once I heard Scott tell him that he did not know what the expedition would do without him . . . Petty Officer Evans and Crean and Lashly were old friends of Scott of *Discovery* days . . . Evans and Lashly had, amongst other risks, been concerned with him in a famous crevasse adventure on the Ferrar Glacier on the West side of McMurdo Sound. Scott and Evans were both precipitated through a snow bridge into an abyss and hung there dangling on the rope in space. It was due to Lashly's resource, strength and presence of mind that they escaped with their lives. Such experiences make for lasting friendship . . . Nobody ever doubted, all through the winter, that Petty Officer Evans would be one of the ones chosen for the Pole . . . The party selected by Captain Scott for the Pole journey were the four men who possessed the most striking personalities."

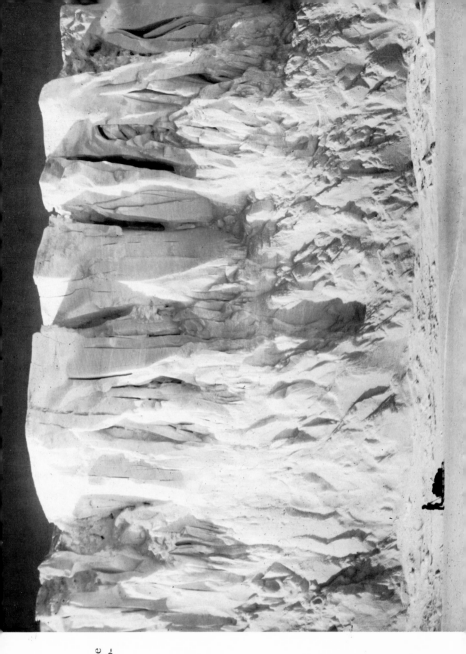

Edge of the ice shelf (*Paul Popper Ltd*)

The Matterhorn Berg and Mt Erebus (*Paul Popper Ltd*)

Scott wrote a good deal about his companions, often in the quiet hours of a spell on night watch: "Of hopeful signs for the future none are more remarkable than the health and spirit of our people. It would be impossible to imagine a more vigorous community, and there does not seem to be a single weak spot in the twelve good men and true who are chosen for the southern advance. All are now experienced sledge travellers, knit together with a bond of friendship that has never been equalled under such circumstances. Thanks to these people, and more especially to Bowers and Petty Officer Evans, there is not a single detail of our equipment which is not arranged with the utmost care and in accordance with the test of experience. It is a really satisfactory state of affairs all round. If the southern journey comes off, nothing, not even priority at the pole, can prevent the expedition ranking as one of the most important that ever entered the polar regions."

He had something to say about all the members of the expedition in his Personal Sketches: "The study of the individual character is a pleasant pastime in such a mixed community of thoroughly nice people, and the study of relationships and interactions is fascinating—men of the most diverse upbringing and experience are really pals with one another." After talking about the officers and scientists he went on: "The men are equally fine. Edgar Evans has proved a useful member of our party; he looks after our sledges and sledge equipment with a care of management and a fertility of resource which is truly astonishing—on trek he is just as sound and hard as ever and has an inexhaustible store of anecdote. Crean is perfectly happy, ready to do anything and go anywhere, the harder the work the better. Evans and Crean are great friends. Lashly is his old self in every respect, hard working to the limit, quiet, abstemious, and determined. You see altogether I have a good set of people with me, and it will go hard if we don't achieve something."

Even the small details came in for appreciative mention, as when the cook was sick: "Clissold's work of cooking has fallen on Hooper and Lashly, and it is satisfactory to find that the various dishes and bread bakings maintain their excellence. It is splendid to have people who refuse to recognize difficulties."

The twelve good men and true chosen for the Southern Advance were the ten pony leaders—Scott, Wilson, Atkinson, Oates, Bowers, Cherry-Garrard, Wright, and Petty Officers Evans, Crean and Keohane—plus Lieutenant Evans and Lashly who were to start as motor party. The subject of the motors was much on Scott's mind as the time for departure drew nearer: "I think our plan will carry us through without the motors (though in that case nothing else must fail), and will take full advantage of such help as the motors may give . . ." And again: "I do not count on the motors—that is a strong point in our case—but should they work well our earlier task of reaching the glacier will be made quite easy. Apart from such help I am anxious that these machines should enjoy some measure of success and justify the time, money, and thought which have been given to their construction. I am still very confident of the possibility of motor traction, whilst realizing that reliance cannot be placed on it in its present untried evolutionary state—it is satisfactory to add that my own view is the most cautious one held in our party. Day is increasingly hopeful about the motors. He is an ingenious person and has been turning up new rollers out of a baulk of oak supplied by Meares and with Simpson's small motor as a lathe. The motors may save the situation, Day is rather more sanguine in temperament than his sledge is reliable in action."

When the motors were brought out for their first trial run one of them bumped down on to the ice over the tide crack and broke the back axle. Day and Lashly repaired it as good as new—"better and stronger," according to Ponting, "I realized that Day and Lashly were men whom nothing could daunt and whose resources and skill were equal to any emergency." Scott added: "Day and Lashly are both hopeful of the machines, and they really ought to do something after all the trouble that has been taken."

With the advent of spring in September all was bustle at Cape Evans. Small parties set out in all directions. Scott went over to the Western mountains for two weeks with Bowers and Petty Officer Evans. Lieutenant Evans, Gran and Petty Officer Forde went to Corner Camp to dig it out. Forde got his hands badly frostbitten which caused Scott some annoyance, when he heard about it, because he thought it was due to carelessness. Evans and Gran completed the survey of McMurdo Sound on their return.

As the departure date for the Pole drew near Scott wrote to his wife. He had left orders that the ship, when it came to relieve them, was to sail again not later than the first week in March. This meant it was unlikely that the Polar party would be able to return home in 1912, because he did not expect to get back till the end of March. So he asked his wife to write to Mrs Lashly and Mrs Evans "in praise of their good men, as indeed I should".

CHAPTER 14

MOTOR PARTY ON THE POLAR JOURNEY

THE ORDERS FOR the motor party were to "proceed at convenient speed to Corner Camp, then to One Ton Depot, and thence due south to latitude 80° 30′ South." Clissold was to have been the fourth member of the motor party because his mechanical aptitude was a considerable asset. But he had to be withdrawn at the last moment because he was not fully recovered from the severe concussion he suffered in a fall on an iceberg while posing for Ponting. His place was taken by Hooper the steward. So the party was Day and Lashly, drivers, with Lieutenant Evans and Hooper as steersmen.

The great journey was due to start on 23rd October, 1911—"but the inevitable little defects cropped up. Day and Lashly spent the afternoon making good these defects in a satisfactory manner," wrote Scott. He thought the weights seemed a good deal heavier than bargained for, and, according to Lashly, each car was to pull 1 ton 8 cwts 10 lbs or a total of 6,290 lbs between them. There were 5 twelve-foot sledges to carry the stores, pony food and petrol and a smaller sledge for the party's camping equipment.

A fresh start was made on 24th October. It was not very encouraging. The wooden pattens on the tracks gripped best on hard snow, but just off Cape Evans there was a belt of smooth sea-ice, with only a thin covering of snow. The tracks skidded round on this without moving the loads an inch. They had to lay down sacks and anything else that would help the treads to grip before the party could move off. Scott described it: "The only alarming incident was the slipping of the chains when Day tried to start on some ice very thinly covered with snow. The starting effort on such heavily loaded sledges is very heavy, but I thought the grip of the pattens and studs would have been good enough on any surface. Looking at the place afterwards I found that the studs had grooved the ice. I find myself immensely eager that these tractors should succeed, even though they may not be a very great help to our Southern Advance. A small measure of success will be enough to show their possibilities, their ability to revolutionize Polar transport. A season of experiment with a small workshop at hand may be all that stands between success and failure."

Lashly started a diary as the motor party's march began. It was kept in a "Navigating Officer's Notebook" which was always a much sought after item of stationery for its convenient pocket-book size.

24.10.11 Motor sledges left Cape Evans at 10.30 a.m. Surfac very heavy. Did 3 miles and camped for lunch. After lunch going very heavy. Only made three-quarters of a mile and camped for the night at 9 o'clock. Had to put in one roller.

25.10.11 Low temperature, surface the same. Got engines under way, but with difficulty. Had to drag the sledges up continually and finally relay. Camped at Glacier Tongue at 3.30 for lunch. Went on again after a lot of difficulty and camped on a pretty good surface at 8.30. Had to put in 3 rollers. Mr Simpson and Mr Gran passed us on their way to Hut Point. Surface seems a lot better ahead.

Tryggve Gran asked Lashly: "How goes it with the cars?" Lashly replied: "As expected, sir." Gran explained that what he meant was clear—frostbitten fingers and endless trouble.

26.10.11 Started at 9.30. Engines going well. Surface very much better. Dropped one tin of petrol each and some lubricating oil. Lunched about 2 miles from Hut Point. Captain and supporting party arrived from Cape Evans to help us over blue ice but were not required. Went on again after lunch but were delayed by the other sledge not being able to get along. I am beginning to think the motors are not powerful enough to pull the loads over heavy surfaces as they are continually overheating. The distance in each run is about from a thousand yards to a mile. Then it is necessary to stop at least half an hour if no wind, and in cold a little less. Then again it is most difficult to keep the carburettors warm to start again, but it seems we may overcome this in time, but the overheating we shall not be able to get over all the time. The engine is dragging such heavy loads, or may be, we say such heavy surfaces. We arrived at Hut Point and proceeded to Cape Armitage and were held up by bad weather. We pitched the tent and waited for the other car to come up as she was delayed all the afternoon and could not make any headway. At 6.30 p.m. Mr Bowers and Mr Garrard came out to us and told us to come back to Hut Point for the night when we all enjoyed a good hoosh and a nice night with Mr Meares and Dimitri.

Scott had some more to say about the motors: "It is already evident that had the rollers been metal cased and the runners metal covered they would now be as good as new. I cannot think why we had not the sense to have this done. As things are I am satisfied we have the right men to deal with the difficulties of the situation. The motor programme is not of vital importance to our plan and it is possible the machines will do little to help us, but already they have vindicated themselves."

27.10.11 Came out to cars and got them under way in fairly good time. We got away in fairly good style and seemed to be improving. The surface was better for running on but rough, and the overheating is not overcome yet. Got near the barrier and the engine seems to be giving trouble again. Shall have to overhaul at lunch time. The other car passed us and arrived on the barrier first. We got up on to the barrier and caught up, then we camped for lunch and the trouble began again. We found on opening my crank chamber that the big end brass had gone pot so we decided to put in the spare. Of course this meant time and a cold job but we did it and were ready to proceed again at 10 p.m. But the temperature was low and it seemed we should never start so we camped for the night.

Day and Lashly had been working in a temperature of $-25°$ to put the motor right.

28.10.11 Got on again in the morning. Had some difficulty in starting, but finally got away, but not for long. Our old trouble is with us again and the surface is heavy. There is very little doubt we are in for a hot time as every time I do a run I find it shakes something loose. So it keeps me pretty well employed. The next trouble is my fan got temporarily seized, but not to hurt, only delayed us a short time. We are continually waiting for one another to come up.

Lashly's motor was the one that had been tested in Norway before the expedition started. Overheating had been a problem then and various modifications were made to the cooling system at the Wolseley works. The difficulty was that at the low speeds—about a mile an hour—at which the tractors travelled there was no rush of wind to help the fan cooling. The front two cylinders were cooled adequately by the fan, but the rear two overheated all the time. The designer had had a nasty accident at the Wolseley works and nearly lost his fingers in the fan while trying to modify the air flow. When the engine was stopped to let the rear two cylinders cool, the carburettor also cooled to such an extent that the petrol would no longer vaporize. Blow lamps for warming carburettors were part of the tractor's equipment. Once they were under way the two machines ran at different speeds which meant they leapfrogged along independently of each other and without support. This drawback was well illustrated on the run from the sea ice up the snow slope on to the barrier. Lashly was ahead and going well when he ran out of lubricating oil which was on the other tractor some way behind. So instead of being able to make an unbroken run straight up on to the barrier he had to stop and wait for the other one to catch up. When the lubricating oil duly arrived his engine was cold again and he had to go through the blow lamp routine to get it started. Day in the meantime had managed to run unchecked on to the barrier.

29.10.11 Got away again this morning but had to wait for the other car. She seems to be giving a lot of trouble. I went back to see, the trouble and the chief difficulty is dirty petrol due to putting in a new drum. Anyhow, got her up and camped for lunch. After lunch started again and all seemed to be going well when Mr Day's car gave out at the big end bearing.

30.10.11 Left Mr Day's car and went on. Did seven miles and camped. We are now about 6 miles from Corner Camp.

31.10.11 Got away after some difficulty and did nearly get to Corner Camp, but it came on thick and had to camp.

1.11.11 Started and got away with some difficulty. Passed Corner Camp and broke another crank head brass so this is an end to the motors. Now comes the man-hauling part of the show.

Scott had told Lieutenant Evans that he would be satisfied if the motors got their loads past White Island. Thanks to the determination, skill and perseverance of Day and Lashly they were successful in this.

CHAPTER 15

MAN-HAULING

THE MOTORS HAD dragged their loads for about 51 miles when the motor party became man-haulers. The entry for 1st November, 1911, went on:

> Started after lunch with 190 lbs per man. A strong head wind. Made three miles and camped for the night.

> They got the whole 760 lb load on to one 10-foot sledge and made about one mile an hour.

> 2.11.11 Started again. Surface very heavy. Made 16½ miles and camped.

Day and Hooper were both over 6 feet tall so they pulled in front while Evans and Lashly, shorter and stockier, dragged as wheelers. Evans was determined not to be overtaken by the main party with the ponies and aimed at something between 15 and 17 miles a day. In fact, the main party only started on 1st November, and Scott deliberately kept the marches down to about 10 miles a day to begin with to save the ponies, so there was no real likelihood of the motor party being overtaken. Amundsen at this time was more than 150 miles further south.

Lashly's daily record of the distance marched over the next fortnight never measured up to Evans' expectations. Nevertheless, they were 6 days ahead of the main party.

4.11.11 Started again and the going was a bit easier. Made 13 miles and camped.

5.11.11 Made good 14½ miles and camped. Weather is very good.

From 6th to 15th November Lashly's diary just listed the daily mileage which showed an average of something under 12 miles a day. The dates from 9th to 15th were bracketed together and covered by a general note: "Surface very bad, soft snow with occasional hard patches and sastrugi. Prevailing wind seems to be South-East, surface covered with soft crystals." They had reached One Ton Depot on 9th November and took on the extra loads which had to be taken forward. This put the weight to be dragged up to 205 lbs per man. It was just south of One Ton that they came to soft surfaces—so soft that they sank in nearly a foot at each step. With a full load to pull they were ready to drop at the end of a 10-hour slog.

A note on an otherwise blank page at the back of the diary reads: "14th November, 1911, Lat. 80° 25′ South Long. 169° 22′ East. Many happy returns of the day to my dear wife." The position he gave was just a few miles short of the appointed rendezvous with the main party.

16.11.11 Laid up.

17.11.11
18.11.11 } Still delayed waiting for the party to come along.

While they were waiting they built a huge cairn to mark the depot and called it Mt Hooper after the youngest member of the party. They spent long hours resting peacefully in their sleeping bags while Day read to them from the *Pickwick Papers*.

19.11.11 Sunday. No ponies arrived.

20.11.11 No sign of the party yet.

21.11.11 Ponies arrived at 5 o'clock and marched on another 3½ miles and camped, having done 13 miles geographical.

It was 5 o'clock in the morning that they arrived because they had been marching at night, although, of course, it was still light, to give the ponies the best conditions for rest in the day time. The party had been held up for a day by a blizzard at Corner Camp and had had one day's rest at One Ton Depot, after meeting head winds most of the way. The motor party broke camp and moved on 3½ miles, so by 10 o'clock in the morning the whole Southern Advance was camped together for the first time. They had travelled 192 miles from Cape Evans.

22.11.11 Marching by night now and 13 miles per march, building cairns on the route every few miles. Surface still soft. Ponies doing very well also dogs. Ours is quite a large transport. Shall commence killing some of the ponies to-morrow I expect as their food will not last.

It was indeed a large transport now, 16 men, 5 tents, 10 ponies, 23 dogs and 13 sledges. Amundsen at this time, with a much smaller transport, was some 300 miles nearer the pole. He had with him 4 men and 4 sledges, with 13 dogs to each sledge. He was covering 20 to 25 miles a day with ease, building a depot at each degree of latitude and giving his dogs a day's rest at each depot. His men rode on the sledges for the first hundred miles and thereafter they were towed along behind on skis. Above all, he was over the unknown hurdle of a route from the barrier to the polar plateau.

The orders for the motor party now were to march ahead of the main party, covering 15 miles a day, and to build cairns to mark the route at roughly 4 mile intervals. With the pony walls that were built to shelter the ponies at the camp sites it ensured that the homeward route would be well marked. Lashly made a note in the middle of his diary to say: "Cairns at lunch camps 2 and at 4 and 3 miles. Pony walls at night camps." It was noticeable that in the colder night temperatures ice crystals formed on the surface which reduced the glide on the sledges to practically nothing.

23.11.11 We are now in the 82nd degree and all seems to be going pretty well. Hope it will continue to do so. Everybody is keen on the job. We are still man-hauling. Mr Day and Hooper return tomorrow. Shot Jehu.

The motor party were hungry by this time as they had been living on the barrier ration, which had been designed for a small expenditure of energy and not for hard man-hauling. Pony meat made a welcome and much needed addition.

24.11.11 Change tents tomorrow. Dr Atkinson joined us today. Day and Hooper cut a sledge in half and started back for Cape Evans. Jehu had been the Doctor's pony so Atkinson made a third at man-hauling.

For the next few days Lashly just noted: "Weather bad, surface bad."

28.11.11 Killed Chinaman. Second pony to go.
29.11.11 Changed tents today. Mr Wright joined us for man-hauling. We are now a complete unit.
30.11.11 Finer again today. Quite close to land.
1.12.11 Clear today. Killed Christopher.

This was Oates's pony, a vicious little beast that had caused endless trouble. However, he cut up well and the man-hauling tent had a nice piece of undercut from him.

2.12.11 Very bad light and warm. Killed Victor.

3.12.11 Blizzard. Did not get away till noon. Did 6 miles and camped. Came on thick.

4.12.11 Got up at 3 a.m. Breakfast and started to catch up to the ponies. Had not been under way long before it started to blizz, but had to get on as we were almost out of food. We were following the tracks of the others but lost them on two occasions and had some difficulty in picking them up. We finally saw the dog camp about ten yards ahead. Then we knew we were all right so we camped and had a lunch and turned in after having a very trying march for 4 miles. At about noon the weather cleared and we saw the land looming up, also the Beardmore which is about 12 miles ahead of us. We did 11 miles and camped for the night.

The Beardmore Glacier at this point stretched across their front to their left. This was the Gateway from the barrier surface to the Polar plateau 10,000 feet above. Scott was aiming for a little tributary, which led up on to the main glacier surface. It avoided some of the worst pressure waves where the main stream met the flat barrier surface.

5.12.11 We are laid up again as there is a very fierce blizzard on again. This of course is a great drawback to us as we are only 12 miles off the Beardmore and we have still got 5 ponies left, and not much food for them. Killed Michael last night. We are eating horse flesh now as we are getting pretty good appetites, and it is quite good.

Amundsen at this time was in 87°–88° and still covering his 25 miles a day.

6.12.11 Blizzard still raging. Very warm. Temperature
   plus 33°.

7.12.11 Blizzard still raging. Temperature very high. Everything getting soaked.

8.12.11 Still laid up.

Soft snow piled high over the route they would have to take
and the remaining ponies lost all condition. They had to be
kept for the last haul on to the glacier, but their food was almost
spent in inactivity. Before this disastrous setback Scott had
hoped that they might still be pulling loads on the lower reaches
of the glacier.

9.12.11 Made a move today. Very heavy going especially for
   the poor ponies. They had their last feed this morning. All
   killed tonight.

It was christened Shambles Camp. Lashly referred to it later
as the Pony Camp. After the next day's march they made the
lower glacier depot. The whole party was man-hauling now
except for the dogs bringing up the rear.

10.12.11 Commenced to climb the glacier. We are all man-
   hauling. The snow is frightfully deep. The dogs are following
   with some of our load.

Scott was vexed by the slow progress. On 10th December,
he wrote in his diary: "Evans's party could not keep up and
Wilson told me some very alarming news about them. It
appears that Atkinson says that Wright is getting played out
and Lashly is not as fit as he was owing to the heavier pulling
since the blizzard. I have not felt satisfied about this party. The
finish of the march today showed clearly that something was

wrong. They fell a long way behind, had to take off skis, and took nearly half an hour to come up a few hundred yards. True the surface was awful and going worse every moment. It is a very serious business if the men are going to crack up. As for myself, I never felt fitter, and my party can easily hold its own." The three remaining man-hauling parties went on to the Summit Ration from this point and started to pick up straight-away, the most marked improvement was apparent in Lashly's condition. The summit ration consisted of 16 ozs biscuit, 12 ozs pemmican, 2 ozs butter, half an ounce of cocoa, 3 ozs sugar and nearly an ounce of tea. This was almost 34½ ozs of food per man, and in addition there was the usual onion powder, curry powder and salt.

Evans and Lashly had been man-hauling for six weeks by this date, whereas the others had only put on harness on the 10th. So, perhaps, the criticism was unjust. Things were a little better on 11th December when Scott said that Evans's party "made heavy weather at first, but when relieved of a little weight and having cleaned their runners and readjusted their load they came on in fine style, and passed us, and took the lead." But they fell back later and earned another rebuke from Scott. On 12th December it was Scott's sledge that had the greatest difficulty in the early part of the day. Evans's team was sent off in advance and Scott could not catch them until the evening camp. The next day they were all in difficulty with appallingly heavy surfaces, sledges sinking in and exhausting efforts being required to break them out and get moving again. Lashly was unruffled by his leaders' tensions and went stolidly on with the back-breaking work.

11.12.11 Still going up the hill. Very heavy going. Very soft snow, no improvement. The dogs are coming on a few more miles. Dogs left us at lunch time having done their work well. The ponies also did well.

His Master's Voice (*Paul Popper Ltd*)

Capt. Scott, Lieut. Bowers, Dr Simpson and P. O. Evans leave on an early spring reconnaissance (*Paul Popper Ltd*)

Bowers had written to Mrs Scott before leaving Cape Evans and his letter touched on the subject of dogs: "Certainly to trust the final dash to such an uncertain element as dogs would be a risky thing, whereas man-haulage though slow, is sure, and I for one am delighted at the decision. After all, it will be a fine thing to do that plateau with man-haulage in these days of the supposed decadence of the British Race." They made the Lower Glacier Depot on 10th December and the dog teams returned to Cape Evans.

12.12.11 Very heavy going. Not much progress, about 4 miles.

A wry comment from Scott at this point: "Here-abouts Shackleton found hard blue ice."

13.12.11 Did better today, about 6 miles.

They were pulling on skis. Without them they sank to their knees in the soft snow. Even so, the sledges sank so deep that the cross-bars underneath were acting as ploughs.

14.12.11 Did much better today, 9 miles.

It was on this day that Amundsen reached the Pole.

15.12.11 Surface still getting better, but had to camp early on account of fog and snow.
16.12.11 Got away very early and did 9½ miles. Came over high pressure ridges. Had to pull up and then toboggan down to the other side.
17.12.11 Got away well and came over some very rough ice, but made good headway, 11 miles.

They were climbing the glacier at a rate of about 500 feet a day but were still not halfway up it. This was the day that Amundsen started for home.

18.12.11 Again we did a good run and found the surface much better. 12¼ miles.

19.12.11 Another good day. 14¾ miles. We are getting well up the glacier. We are about 5,700 feet up above the barrier level.

20.12.11 Good run today. 19 miles 650 yards.

21.12.11 Very heavy going and all up hill. Had to stop for light got so bad, but were able to resume after lunch and did 11 miles 200 yards. Tomorrow we shall be only 8 as 4 are returning.

They made the Upper Glacier Depot and the First Supporting party turned back. This was Dr Atkinson, Cherry-Garrard, Wright and Petty Officer Keohane. They got back to Cape Evans on 28th January, 1912, showing slight signs of scurvy. Scott had been watching the individual performance of each man on the way up the glacier. He congratulated himself later on that he had kept the right 8 men with him. The two parties left now were: Scott, Wilson, Oates and Petty Officer Evans on one sledge, with Lieutenant Evans, Bowers, Lashly and Crean on the other.

22.12.11 Still going up. We are now leaving the land. Made a depot this morning, and said farewell to the returning party. Did 11 miles with full load again. Surface very good. Temperature lower, altitude 7,100 feet.

23.12.11 Got away at 7.50 and soon got into some very bad crevasses which troubled us most of the day, but covered 15 miles. Temperature getting lower, we are getting minus night and day.

24.12.11 Christmas Eve. We have had a good day, but pretty heavy dragging up slopes nearly all day. Distance covered 14 miles due South. We are now on our proper course for the Pole as far as we can see. Tomorrow is Christmas Day.

Monday, 25th December, 1911, was an eventful day. Bowers was the cook in Lashly's tent for the week. He was also the commissariat officer. He marked the occasion with the addition of a little pony meat to the breakfast ration. Then Lashly took up the story:

25.12.11 Good day. Made good 15 miles. Very bad crevasses. I went down one full length of my harness and was hauled up again. The thing was about 50 feet deep and 8 feet wide, and 120 feet long. Rather a ghastly sight while dangling in one's harness. We had a good dinner at night. Pemmican, chocolate eclair, pony meat, plum pudding and crystallized ginger, and caramels. Could not hardly move.

Bowers gave a fuller account: "About the middle of the morning we were all falling in continually, but Lashly in my team had the worst drop. He fell to the length of his harness and the trace. I was glad that having noticed his rope rather worn, I had given him a new one a few days before. He jerked Crean and me off our feet backwards, and Crean's harness being jammed under the sledge, which was half across an eight-feet bridge (it was a 12-foot sledge, and it only just bridged the gap) he could do nothing. I was a little afraid of sledge and all going down, but fortunately the crevasse ran diagonally. We could not see Lashly for a great overhanging piece of ice was over him. Teddy Evans and I cleared Crean and we all three got Lashly up with the Alpine rope cut into the snow sides which overhung the hole. We then got the sledge into safety.

"Today is Lashly's birthday; he is married and has a family; is forty-four years of age, and due for his pension from the service. He is as strong as most and is an undefeated old sportsman. Being a Chief Stoker, R.N., his original job was charge of one of the ill-fated motor sledges."

Scott, too, described the incident at some length: "Then we started up a rise, and to our annoyance found ourselves amongst crevasses once more—very hard smooth névé between the ridges at the edge of crevasses, and therefore very difficult to get foothold to pull the sledges. Got our ski sticks out, which improved matters, but we had to tack a good deal and several of us went half down. After half an hour of this I looked round and found the second sledge halted some way in rear—evidently someone had gone into a crevasse. We saw the rescue work going on, but had to wait half an hour for the party to come up, and got mighty cold. It appears that Lashly went down very suddenly, nearly dragging the crew with him. The sledge ran on and jammed the span so that the Alpine rope had to be got out and used to pull Lashly to the surface again. Lashly says the crevasse was 50 feet deep and 8 feet cross, in form U, showing that the word 'unfathomable' can rarely be applied. Lashly is 44 today and as hard as nails. His fall has not even disturbed his equanimity."

Scott, too, added a note about the Christmas dinner: "We had 4 courses. The first, pemmican, full whack, with slices of horse meat flavoured with onion and curry powder and thickened with biscuit, then an arrowroot, cocoa and biscuit hoosh sweetened; then a plum pudding; then cocoa with raisins, and finally a dessert of caramels and ginger. After the feast it was difficult to move. Wilson and I couldn't finish our share of plum pudding. We all slept splendidly and feel thoroughly warm—such is the effect of full feeding."

With the Christmas festivities behind them they were on the

trail again, but as Lieutenant Evans observed: "A man trained to watch over men's health, over athletes' training, perhaps, would have seen something amiss. The two teams soon lost their springy step, the sledges dragged more slowly, and we gazed ahead almost wistfully. Yes, the strain was beginning to tell, though none of us would have confessed it." He and Lashly had pulled a loaded sledge over 600 miles by this time, and all of them had marched that distance.

26.12.11 Made good 13 miles again. Surface very heavy and dragging is heavy.

27.12.11 Another good day. Made good 13 miles. Surface is very changeful. Some very bad crevasses for about an hour.

28.12.11 Another good day. Made good 13 miles. Surface very heavy. Had a job to get the sledge along.

29.12.11 Sledges going heavy still. We still get that nasty head wind. Made good 12 miles.

30.12.11 Sledges going heavy. Depoted our skis tonight. To-morrow we march in the forenoon and change the sledges into 10 foot. Did 10 miles.

This was the Three Degree Depot.

31.12.11 Did 7 miles and camped to do sledges. Took us till 11 p.m. This is the last of the old year.

During this operation Petty Officer Evans cut his hand rather badly.

1.1.12 We commence our New Year today. Did not get away before 10 o'clock. Did 11 miles. The temperature and wind still troublesome. We are now ahead of Shackleton's dates and have passed the 87th parallel.

2.1.12 Still heavy going. Made good 11 miles.

At this point Scott decided on the final composition of the Polar Party. On Wednesday, 3rd January, he wrote: "Last night I decided to reorganize and this morning told Teddy Evans, Lashly and Crean to return. They are disappointed but take it well." A significant fact was that Bowers had depoted his skis at Three Degree Depot on 30th December. From now on he would have to make his own pace in Scott's five man party, between the other men pulling on skis.

It was soon after this that Scott made a long entry in his diary setting down his appreciation of all the good work done by Petty Officer Evans: "A giant worker with a really remarkable head-piece. It is only now I realize how much has been due to him. Our ski shoes and crampons have been absolutely indispensable, and if the original ideas were not his, the details of manufacture and design and the good workmanship are his alone. He is responsible for every sledge, every sledge fitting, tents, sleep-ing bags, harness, and when one cannot record a single expres-sion of dissatisfaction with any of these items, it shows what an invaluable assistant he has been. Now, besides superin-tending the putting up of the tent, he thinks out and arranges the packing of the sledge; it is extraordinary how neatly and handily everything is stowed, and how much study has been given to preserving the suppleness and good running qualities of the machine. On the barrier before the ponies were killed, he was ever roaming round, correcting faults of stowage."

3.1.12 Very heavy going. The Captain told us this morning we should return tomorrow. That is if they can get along with the load, Mr Evans, myself and Crean. Captain Scott, Captain Oates, Dr Wilson, Mr Bowers and Evans, these are the people going on to the Pole. Today has been a very cold wind and low drift, but we have done 12 miles.

4.1.12 Homeward bound. Said goodbye to party at 10 a.m. and made off at 10.45 ourselves. Covered 13 miles. Very fine.

CHAPTER 16

LAST SUPPORTING PARTY

ON THURSDAY 4th January Scott wrote: "The second party had followed us in case of accident, but as soon as I was certain we could get along we stopped and said farewell . . . poor old Crean wept and even Lashly was affected."

After the first day's homeward march Lieutenant Evans employed a dodge to make longer marching hours. Before getting up in the morning he would secretly advance his watch an hour, putting it back again when he got the opportunity during the day. Lashly said afterwards that he and Crean were perfectly well aware that the ruse was being practised, but they entered into the spirit of it and never let on. It was in the interests of all three to make long marches, because it was cutting it very fine to attempt the 800 mile return march with only three men.

5.1.12 Did 17 miles. Rather warm. Surface not very good.

6.1.12 Picked up the depot at noon and the ski at night camp.

7.1.12 Very good day. Did 16½ miles on skis. A cold wind behind us. Much better than in front.

8.1.12 Blizzard blowing but we could manage to march with difficulty. Did 13 miles.

9.1.12 Travelling very difficult. Bad light and blizzing. Did about 12 miles. Seems a bit better tonight.

10.1.12 Still very bad light and drifting snow but we have to push on as we are still a long way from the depot, but we hope to reach it before we run out of provisions.

11.1.12 A bit better today. Did about 14 miles.

The bad visibility and blizzard had caused them to lose the outward track and instead of arriving at the top of the Beardmore Glacier they found themselves faced with the Shackleton Ice Falls. The choice was a three-day detour round the Ice Falls or the direct descent. They decided to risk it to save precious time and food.

It was a frightening descent. The loaded sledge took charge and glissaded over yawning crevasses, but, as Lashly had done nine years before, they came through with no bones broken.

12.1.12 Did a good day but came over some very rough surface and plenty of crevasses. We are camped in a very rough spot tonight. Looks very rough ahead, but we must try and get through it as the depot can't be more than a day's march away. Did about 17 miles.

13.1.12 Had a long march and a very rough one. Plenty of crevasses and ice falls. Did not reach depot. Made good about 10 miles.

14.1.12 Sunday. Reached the Mount Darwin Depot at 2 p.m. Camped and replenished our food supply. Had lunch and commenced to descend the glacier. We are finding it a bit warmer tonight. It is plus one. The temperature on the summit has been minus all the time.

15.1.12 Had a good run today but rough ice, crevasses, plenty, with crampons on.

16.1.12 Had a good run today, but we are camped in a very bad place tonight, but hope to get out of it tomorrow early, and if possible reach the Cloudmaster Depot.

17.1.12 Have had a very bad day. It took us all day to get clear of the pressure, but we are out of it now. But have not been able to reach the depot. Don't want many days like this.

But the next day was just as bad. Low cloud and bad visibility caused them to miss the hard blue ice of the main glacier stream and, once more, they found themselves amongst ice falls and gaping crevasses. Most of the snow and the snow bridges had disappeared under the influence of the rays of the summer sun. At one crevasse they crossed by a V-shaped ridge. Lashly in the lead, had to sit astride the bridge and ease himself over. Evans and Crean sat face to face at either end of the sledge balancing it while Lashly hauled in on the rope.

18.1.12 Got on the move again but did not get far before we were in worse pressure than ever. Don't want another day like this. We reached the depot at 11 p.m. half a day late and very tired after 12 hours heavy slogging.

This was the Cloudmaker Depot.

Evans had had his goggles off all day to pick out the course over the crevasses and he suffered agonies of snow blindness for the next fortnight. He was unable to write his diary up again until 29th January. He was too blind to do any useful pulling and could only walk along beside the sledge.

19.1.12 Today we got away and made a better start, but came on to a very soft snow during the afternoon. Camped at 7 p.m. Mr Evans very snow blind, and we could not make progress as there is only two of us. But we must push on tomorrow and reach the next depot as soon as possible. 11 miles.

At this point Lashly skipped some pages and started another section further on in which he made additional entries on days when there was anything to report on Evans's health. The second entry for 19th January goes on:

19.1.12 Mr Evans snow blind. Did 11½ miles and camped.

20.1.12 Did not get away very smart but we are determined to try and do better than yesterday, and I think we succeeded as we covered over 20 miles on ski. The surface being very soft and knee deep all the time.

20.1.12 (second entry) Mr Evans very bad with blindness. Could not see at all, but we had an excellent surface for skiing, the best I have ever had. So we made the best of it, and done about 21 miles.

21.1.12 Sunday. Had a good day and reached the depot at 6.45 p.m. Tomorrow we hope to get out on the barrier.

21.1.12 (second entry) Mr E. still blind, but a little better. Reached depot in good time.

This was the Lower Glacier Depot.

22.1.12 Got off the glacier today and arrived at Pony depot, changed sledges. We also got a bit of meat and commenced the track across the barrier. We now have got 360 miles to get to Hut Point, geographical miles.

22.1.12 (second entry) Arrived at Pony depot and camped. Fitted mast with bamboos for sail. Took a little meat and changed sledge and proceeded.

They had left three ten foot sledges at this Depot on the outward march because it was expected that the sledges would be badly knocked about on the descent of the glacier.

23.1.12 Made a very good day. Surface very good. Did about 14 miles.

23.1.12 (second entry) Mr Evans all right again.

With the announcement that Mr Evans was all right

again there was no additional medical bulletin until 27th January.

24.1.12 Did a good run today and a good surface. The weather is very warm.

25.1.12 Got away in very thick weather. The surface was very wet and dragging heavy. Stopped to lunch and the wind sprang up so we kept up a very good speed for an hour when it changed to a blizzard and a very wet one. We managed to reach the depot when it eased a bit. It was plus 36° and raining but did not last long.

26.1.12 This have been a wonderful day for surface. This morning we started with a fair wind and a soft snow and a very high temperature—plus 34°—much too high for sledging. We were on skis, or it might have been on stilts for the amount of snow clogging on them. But we were assisted by our sail and did 13 miles—8 of them in the afternoon.

27.1.12 A good run this morning on ski. Took the sledge along with a good breeze and the sail up. No need to pull her, only keep her straight. Did 14½ miles but it was so very hot anyone could take off all clothes and march. Of course it is too hot for this part of the world. But we shall soon get colder weather now.

27.1.12 (second entry) Mr E. suffering from looseness of the bowels.

28.1.12 Today have been rather a heavy drag. The snow is still very soft, and the sun is very hot. It fairly scorches the face, but I am glad to say it is a bit cooler generally. Did 12½ miles. Only another few Sundays and we hope to be safely housed at Cape Evans. We have been out 97 days.

28.1.12 (second entry) Mr E. still suffering from looseness of the bowels.

29.1.12 Another good day. Was helped by the sail all day. One man could manage for about 2 hours. Weather still warm plus 20. Did 16½ miles—14 to next depot.

29.1.12 (second entry) Still suffering from same. Have stopped pemmican for a day or two to see if any improvement, and gave him a little brandy. He is taking some chalk and opium pills.

30.1.12 Very bad light, but fair wind. Picked up depot in evening, did 14 miles. Only two more depots to pick up now. (Second entry) Mr Evans recovered somewhat from looseness but complained of slight stiffness at back of knees.

There was a gap of several pages just before the second entry for 30th January which contained various notes and a table of distances. These were all in geographical miles which Lashly always used.

Cape Evans to	13½ miles	Hut Point
Hut Point to	30 miles	Corner Camp
Corner Camp to	89 miles	One Ton Depot
One Ton Depot to	61 miles	'A' Depot (Mt Hooper)
'A' Depot to	65 miles	'B' Depot (Middle Barrier Depot)
'B' Depot to	73 miles	'C' Depot (Southern Barrier Depot)
'C' Depot to	48 miles	'D' Depot (Lower Glacier Depot)
'D' Depot to	52 miles	Cloudmaker Depot
Cloudmaker Depot to	57 miles	Mount Darwin (Upper Glacier Depot)
Mount Darwin to	120 miles	Three Degree Depot
Three Degree Depot to	192 miles	Pole

This made a total distance from Cape Evans to the Pole of

about 920 statute miles. He tabulated the distance marched each day in miles and hundreds of yards and, besides the note on cairns, there was a little diagram of cairns and pony walls which was evidently not much help. He only kept it up for four days march.

31.1.12 Another very good run today, but light bad. Had again to steer by compass, but it is clear again tonight. The temperature is still high, plus 20 in the day and 10 at night. Did 13 miles.

(Second entry) Stiffness still going on.

1.2.12 Had a very fine day and a heavy pull, but we did 19 miles. Myself and Mr Evans have been out 100 days today. I was forced to change places with my shirts tonight. The under one taking place of the top one.

(Second entry) Still stiff.

As far as shirts were concerned, the two he always wore made four shirts as each side did duty next to the skin for a month. This was a perfectly sensible hygienic arrangement in a climate where clothes got greasy but not dirty.

2.2.12 A very bad light again today. Could not make much progress, but did about 11 miles.

(Second entry) Still stiff.

3.2.12 Again a very bad light, but we got away all right with a bit of wind to help. But the light remained very bad and it came on to bliz just as we camped. Did 13 miles. One more day to next depot.

(Second entry) Still stiff but not improving.

4.2.12 Started in splendid weather. The surface was very bad and dragging very heavy, but it improved as the day went on, and we arrived at the depot at 7.40 p.m. We are now 180

miles from Hut Point and this is Sunday night. We hope to be only two more Sundays on the barrier.
(Second entry) Arrived at depot. No improvement but worse if anything.

This was the Mt Hooper Depot where they had waited for the main party to catch up on the outward march.

5.2.12 Had a fine day and a good light all day. Did not get away till 9 o'clock but did 11½ miles. It is gradually getting colder.
(Second entry) Got away in fine weather. I am beginning to suspect something is wrong with Mr Evans.

6.2.12 Another fine day but the sun was very hot and caused us to sweat a good deal. But we don't mind we are pretty used to such changes. We shall soon be looking for land ahead which will be Mount Discovery, also Mount Erebus. We have 155 miles to go to Hut Point. Did a good run today, 13½ miles. Good.
(Second entry) Getting along pretty well, but looseness of the bowels has come on Mr E. again. Stopped his pemmican.

7.2.12 A very fine day but heavy going. We are bringing the land in sight now. The weather has been simply lovely. Did 12 miles.
(Second entry) Got away all right but Mr E. is getting worse. I am almost afraid to think of it. But he is pretty plucky to keep up as he do.

8.2.12 Today have been very favourable and fine. We had a good breeze and set sail after lunch. Did 13 miles. Good. Tomorrow we hope to reach One Ton Depot.
(Second entry) Today Mr Evans no better and is passing blood, not a good sign. It is a job for him to get on his ski now.

9.2.12 A very fine day and quite warm. Reached the depot at

5.5 p.m. and had a good feed of oatmeal. This is our last port of call before reaching Hut Point. We now have 120 miles to go.

(Second entry) Mr Evans same as yesterday, passing blood. But we have reached One Ton Depot and got a change of food which I hope will put him right.

10.2.12 Did a good march in very thick weather. Tonight we are camped and I am sorry to say Mr Evans is suffering from scurvy and very badly. Of course we knew this, but we have had to get along and not look at the bad side. But the time have come when we must take the greatest care of him. One thing, we have got a change of food and this might improve things, at least we hope so. I am pleased to say myself and Crean are in good health so far thank God. Did 12 miles.

(Second entry) Left One Ton Depot in very thick weather. Had to put Mr Evans on his ski this morning. Had a look at his legs this morning and have come to the conclusion he have got scurvy and bad. Things don't look any too bright for us. Looseness of the bowels gone off, but it is weakening him a lot.

11.2.12 Today before leaving built a cairn and left all gear we could do without, as we must try to get along as fast as possible. It is very bad light on starting, cleared a while during the day, but came on to bliz just before 6.30. We had to camp. Did about 11 miles. We are about 99 miles from Hut Point.

(Second entry) Today no improvement in Mr Evans, but worse. So we have left behind gear. I am giving him oatmeal and seal liver and meat out of the pemmican and other changes of food as we have got. We found on looking at the box of sledge biscuits we brought along that through being stowed with snow on top that the snow has melted and run into the box and spoilt all our biscuit, or nearly all of them. This is the second time it has happened. This have put us in a bad state, but we must manage somehow.

12.2.12 Did not get away until 10 o'clock on account of bad weather. But it turned out a fine day and we did about 7 miles. But the surface was very heavy and dragging rather stiff for us as there is only the two of us now. Mr Evans is getting along as best he can on ski. I hope he will be able to keep on his legs.

(Second entry) Mr Evans went on ahead part of the day. We have got to lift him on to the skis now and help him about. It is nearly come to a climax. We shall soon have to drag him.

13.2.12 Got away in good time. Put Mr Evans on his skis and sent him on slowly. The surface was very bad all day, but nice and fine. Progress is slow, but we can't expect too fast with two.

14.2.12 Started this morning but had to stop and dump everything we possibly could and take Mr Evans on the sledge. We still have about 70 miles to go. No doubt we shall have our work cut out, but we must try and do our best to get to Hut Point in safety.

Evans was completely helpless by this time and quite unable to stand. He told Lashly and Crean to leave him in his sleeping bag and go on without him. He said afterwards that it was the only occasion in his naval career that an order of his had been disobeyed. Thinking the end was near he wrote a message which was in Lashly's possession for many years afterwards:

> 14th Feb.
> About 44 miles
> S 3° E of
> Corner Camp.

E. R. G. R. Evans unable to stand or walk, attempted to proceed on ski but was delaying sledge besides being in great pain. Lashly and Crean counselled putting Evans on sledge and made depot of everything not necessary for existence. Party now proceeding to Corner Camp.

E. R. G. R. Evans.

Lashly had done some geologizing on the descent of the Beardmore and had brought along some rock samples which he unloaded and left here along with their skis.

15.2.12 Started in fine weather this morning but it soon became thick and progress became rather slow. But after a while the sun came out and we were able to put in a good march, the sail helping us a good deal.

16.2.12 Today has been a very heavy drag for us. The light is still very bad. We saw Castle Rock today, also Observation Hill, but they are a long way off. Today we have had to reduce our ration to one half nearly as we cannot possibly reach Hut Point for another four days.

17.2.12 Today it has been thick again, but we could see the land and get along, and the sail helped us a bit. We arrived at the motor and camped. We are now 30 miles from Hut Point. Mr Evans is getting worse but we must try and get him along although it is hard slogging and we are not so strong as we might be after our long pull.

18.2.12 Started to move Mr Evans this morning, but he collapsed and fainted right away. Got him round again and used the last drop of brandy. Put him on the sledge after a while and got away although he is pretty bad. But found the hauling so heavy we decided to camp and Crean proceed on foot to Hut Point and get relief in some shape. He left here about 9 a.m. the distance 30 miles geographical. I made a trip to Corner Camp and got some butter and cheese, and also back to the motor and got more oil in case of bad weather. This being an ideal day and I hope it will keep clear for Crean to reach Hut Point in safety.

19.2.12 Today Mr Evans is a bit cheerful and I think a little better. The rest will do good and help him to get the other part of the journey over. It was very thick and cold this morning but cleared as the day advanced.

The entries in Lashly's diary stopped here, as he and Evans settled down to wait for help to arrive. But first he took one more precaution as the weather was still thick. He collected a large piece of black cloth from the broken down motor and rigged it like a flag over their sledge to attract attention.

Crean had a walk of 34 statute miles to reach Hut Point. They had depoted their skis to save weight so he had the additional hazard of traversing the crevassed area round White Island on foot, without skis to spread the weight, and with nobody to help him if he went through a bridge. His only food was a little chocolate and a few biscuits. After marching for 18 hours he arrived at 3.30 a.m. at the hut at Hut Point, delirious with exhaustion. Half an hour later a blizzard came down. Dr Atkinson and Dimitri were at Hut Point with the dogs, but there was no possibility of starting out for Corner Camp until the blizzard let up the next afternoon. Then, still in drift and bad visibility, uncertain of their position, they made a fast run out to Corner Camp. In a temporary lull Dimitri spotted the black flag on the sledge and Atkinson took over the care of Lashly's patient. The Doctor was lost in admiration for Lashly's care and nursing of Evans. Other doctors have said that they have never read better "non-medical" case histories than Lashly kept of Evans's condition.

They had to wait another night before the weather improved enough to make a start back with Evans on a sledge. Then they made a fast run back to Hut Point with only one short stop.

Lashly took it in turns with Atkinson to ride on the sledge, and, between rides, he was still fit and strong enough to walk and run beside the sledge, often sinking to his knees in the soft surface left by the blizzard.

CHAPTER 17

THE SEARCH

BACK AT Cape Evans for the second winter Lashly was in charge of the mules that had been brought down by the ship on its last visit. Anton, the groom, had gone home and the job fell naturally to Lashly, as he thought at first, till Captain Oates got back from the Pole. But by the end of March the Polar Party were overdue and presumed lost. Before saying goodbye to Scott Lashly had asked to be allowed to return to Hut Point to be there to greet the returning Polar party. Scott had agreed provided there were no mules at Cape Evans for him to look after.

There was speculation as to what could have happened to the Polar Party. In the *Worst Journey* Cherry-Garrard said: "I had a long talk with Lashly, who asked me what I candidly thought had happened to the Southern Party. I told him a crevasse. He says he does not think so; he thinks it is scurvy. Talking about crevasses, he says that, on the return of the Second Return Party they came right over the ice-falls south of Mount Darwin—descending about 2,000 feet into a great valley, down which they travelled towards the west, and so to the Upper Glacier Depot. I believe Scott told Evans (Lieut.) that he meant to come back this same way.

"Then the stuff they got into above the Cloudmaker must have been horrible! Why, there are places where you could put St Paul's into, and that's no exaggeration, neither, and they spent two nights in it. All the way down to the Gateway he says there were crevasses, great big fellows thirty feet across, which

149

we of the First Return Party had crossed both going and coming back, and which we never saw. But then much of the snow had gone and they were visible. Lieutenant Evans was very badly snow blind most of the time. Then outside the Gateway on the barrier, they crossed many crevasses and some had fallen in where we had passed over them.

"Lashly thinks it would be practically impossible for five men to disappear down a crevasse. Where three men got through (and he said it would be impossible to get worse stuff than they came through) five men would be still better off. This is not my view, however. I think that the extra weight of one man might make all the difference in crossing a big crevasse; and if several men fell through one of those great bridges when sledge and men were all on it, I do not think the bridge would hold the sledge."

Lashly and Crean were brought into the councils of the officers when plans for the coming sledging season were discussed. They were listened to with the greatest respect. Both were of the opinion that the Polar Party had been overtaken by scurvy.

The final decision as to what to do in October rested squarely on Dr Atkinson's shoulders. He was the only Naval Officer left in the party—all the others were missing except Lieutenant Evans who had been sent home sick. Besides the Polar party, who must be dead, there was Lieutenant Campbell's party who might still be alive. These six men had originally been landed at Cape Adare after finding Amundsen in the Bay of Whales. On the ship's next visit they had been moved down the coast a little to find better sledging country for exploration. They had gone ashore prepared for a short stay only, but the ship had been unable to take them off again, so they had been stranded for the winter. If they had been able to survive the winter they would be relieved by the ship on its next visit very soon after a relief party could get to them over land, but days might make the difference. On the other hand, if they had survived the winter, they might well be able to make their own way back to Cape Evans.

The Polar party's outward route was known for certain only as far as the top of the Beardmore Glacier. If they had gone into a crevasse on the glacier, or even on the barrier just clear of the Gateway there would be no chance of finding them. How far Lashly's insistence that they had been overtaken by scurvy swayed Atkinson is impossible to say, but the only chance of finding them lay in running across traces of them somewhere along the route.

Atkinson decided to go south on this small chance. After weighing all the argument he decided it was a duty they owed to the expedition to complete the record—success or failure. It was also a duty to the relatives of those lost. Above all his decision was the vital link in the history of British Antarctic exploration that stretched unbroken through Ross, Hooker, Scott and Shackleton, to Scott again.

Lashly had the mules in first class condition when the sledging season came round again in October, 1912. He had also manufactured an ingenious sledge-meter to replace the original ones lost or broken on the Polar journey. This was made of an old bicycle wheel from one of the experimental trucks they had and it served very well.

The mule party set out on the Search journey on 29th October, 1912, and reached Hut Point the same day. They kept up a good pace all the time and got to One Ton Depot on 11th November.

The next day they marched on south, Wright out ahead with the mule party, and the dogs following behind. Eleven miles south of One Ton Depot Wright struck out right-handed by himself and the whole mule party swerved to follow him. He had seen a single bamboo sticking up out of the snow near one of the last season's camps.

As Atkinson's dog team caught up with the mules he took Lashly on his sledge over to where Wright was standing by a mound of snow. Someone brushed the snow away from a little projection which was the ventilation of the tent. Below it was the door.

Atkinson crawled in through the door and had Lashly follow him in. In the words of Tryggve Gran: "Atkinson took Lashly with him into the tent because Lashly was the oldest of us all and the last to have seen Scott and the missing members of the Polar Party. When he came out Lashly did not say a word but tears were rolling from his eyes. No one took the tragedy more to heart than this good natured and faithful man." The bodies of Scott, Wilson and Bowers were inside.

The diaries which were found under the head of Scott's sleeping bag told them the story of the Polar march. Atkinson gathered the whole party together to read them the account of Oates's gallant death and Scott's immortal "Message to the public".

"The Death of Captain Oates

"Friday, March 16 or Saturday, 17th. Lost track of dates, but think the last correct. Tragedy all along the line. At lunch, the day before yesterday, poor Titus Oates said he couldn't go on; he proposed we should leave him in his sleeping bag. This we could not do, and we induced him to come on, on the afternoon march. In spite of its awful nature for him he struggled on and we made a few miles. At night he was worse and we knew the end had come.

"Should this be found I want these facts recorded. Oates' last thoughts were of his mother, but immediately before he took pride in thinking that his regiment would be pleased with the bold way in which he met his death. We can testify to his bravery. He has borne intense suffering for weeks without complaint, and to the very last was able and willing to discuss outside subjects. He did not—would not—give up hope till the very end. He was a brave soul. This was the end. He slept through the night before last hoping not to wake; but he woke in the morning—yesterday. It was blowing a blizzard. He said, 'I am just going outside and may be some time.' He went out into the blizzard and we have not seen him since.

"I take this opportunity of saying that we have stuck to our sick companions to the last. In the case of Edgar Evans, when absolutely out of food and he lay insensible, the safety of the remainder seemed to demand his abandonment, but Providence mercifully removed him at this critical moment. He died a natural death, and we did not leave him till two hours after his death; we knew that poor Oates was walking to his death, but though we tried to dissuade him, we knew it was the act of a brave man and an English gentleman. We all hope to meet the end with a similar spirit, and assuredly the end is not far."

"Message to the Public

"The causes of the disaster are not due to faulty organization, but to misfortune in all risks which had to be undertaken.

"1. The loss of pony transport in March, 1911, obliged me to start later than I had intended, and obliged the limits of stuff transported to be narrowed.

"2. The weather throughout the outward journey, and especially the long gale in 83° S., stopped us.

"3. The soft snow in lower reaches of glacier again reduced pace.

"We fought these untoward events with a will and conquered, but it cut into our provision reserve.

"Every detail of our food supplies, clothing and depots made on the interior ice sheet and over that long stretch of 700 miles to the Pole and back worked out to perfection. The advance party would have returned to the glacier in fine form and with surplus of food, but for the astonishing failure of the man whom we had least expected to fail. Edgar Evans was thought the strongest man of the party.

"The Beardmore Glacier is not difficult in fine weather, but on our return we did not get a single completely fine day; this with a sick companion enormously increased our anxieties.

"As I have said elsewhere we got into frightfully rough ice, and Edgar Evans received a concussion of the brain—he died a natural death, but left us a shaken party, with the season unduly advanced.

"But all the facts above enumerated were as nothing to the surprise which awaited us on the Barrier. I maintain that our arrangements for returning were quite adequate, and that no one in the world would have expected the temperatures and surfaces which we encountered at this time of the year. On the summit in Latitude 85° 86° we had – 20° – 30°. On the Barrier in Latitude 82° 10,000 feet lower we had – 30° in the day, –47° at night pretty regularly, with continuous head wind during our day marches. It is clear that these circumstances come on very suddenly, and our wreck is certainly due to this sudden advent of severe weather, which does not seem to have any satisfactory cause. I do not think human beings ever came through such a month as we have come through, and we should have got through in spite of the weather but for the sickening of a second companion, Captain Oates, and a shortage of fuel in our depots, for which I cannot account, and finally, but for the storm which has fallen on us within 11 miles of the depot at which we hoped to secure our final supplies. Surely misfortune could scarcely have exceeded this last blow. We arrived within 11 miles of our old One Ton Camp with fuel for one last meal and food for two days. For four days we have been unable to leave the tent—the gale howling about us. We are weak, writing is difficult, but for my own sake I do not regret this journey, which has shown that Englishmen can endure hardships, help one another and meet death with as great a fortitude as ever in the past. We took risks, we knew we took them; things have come out against us, and therefore we have no cause for complaint, but bow to the will of Providence, determined still to do our best to the last. But if we have been willing to give our lives to this enterprise, which is for the honour of our country, I appeal to our countrymen to see that those who depend on us are properly cared for.

"Had we lived, I should have had a tale to tell of the hardihood, endurance, and courage of my companions which would have stirred the heart of every Englishman. These rough notes and our dead bodies must tell the tale, but surely, surely a great rich country like ours will see that those who are dependent on us are properly provided for.

(Signed) R. Scott."

Then Atkinson read the burial service over the three, and they built a cairn over the tent. Lashly fashioned a cross from Gran's skis and this was placed on top of the cairn.

Atkinson said he could not find any trace of scurvy in the bodies and put the cause of death down to starvation—"exposure and want" was the phrase used in the first communiqué. A subsequent analysis of the Polar party's rations, after the First World War, showed that they must have been suffering from vitamin deficiency to such an extent as to cause a serous loss of vital energy.

After a fruitless search further south for the body of Oates, the party turned north again for the last time. In the words of Atkinson's report: "On the second day we came again to the resting place of the three and bade them a final farewell. There alone in their greatness they will lie without change or bodily decay with the most fitting tomb in the world above them." On the 21st they found Lashly's depot of gear that he had made on 14th February. The skis were still sticking up out of the snow, drifted to within six inches of the shoes. Lashly's geological specimens were there, and these, together with a roll of film, were collected up and brought back. They got to Cape Evans at the end of November, and found, to their great joy, that Lieutenant Campbell's party had got back safely.

The *Terra Nova* arrived on the 18th January, 1913, to take them home. They lost no time in getting their gear on board, but first there was one last service to be rendered to their dead companions. The ship's carpenter made a great cross of Australian jarrah wood and, at considerable risk to themselves because the ice was very thin, all the members of the Search Party sledged it ashore to Hut Point. From there they took it up and erected it on the top of Observation Hill looking out over the barrier. It still stands there today. On the cross were carved the names of the five men who died and the last line of Tennyson's poem Ulysses:

"To strive, to seek, to find, and not to yield."

CHAPTER 18

EPILOGUE

THE NEWS WAS telegraphed home in February, 1913, when the *Terra Nova* reached New Zealand. It made a tremendous impression throughout the civilized world. President Taft sent a message of condolence to King George V. The King attended a memorial service in St Paul's Cathedral on Friday, 14th February, 1913. Seats were only reserved for the Royal Party and relatives of those lost, but the Cathedral was full, and one newspaper estimated that 10,000 people had to stand outside.

The survivors went to an investiture at Buckingham Palace in July. Lashly and Crean were awarded the Albert Medal for saving the life of Lieutenant Evans on the return of the last Supporting Party. Ponting showed his films at the Palace and the King expressed the hope that it might be possible for all British boys to see them—"as the story of the Scott Expedition could not be known too widely among the youth of the nation, for it would help to promote the spirit of adventure that had made the Empire." Commander (as he then was) Evans and Lashly went to the Royal Naval College, Osborne, to lecture to the cadets on the Expedition. It was received with wild enthusiasm and Evans and Lashly were the heroes of the hour.

Lashly stayed on as shipkeeper in the *Terra Nova* until October when he was discharged to pension. He had always intended to join the Royal Fleet Reserve, but, because he was in the Antarctic, he had been unable to do so at the appropriate time. So a special case was made for him and he enrolled on

11th October, 1913, the day after his discharge from the Royal Navy. Because of this he had no time to take up his employment with the Board of Trade in Cardiff before he was recalled for service on 2nd August, 1914. Almost immediately he joined H.M.S. *Irresistible* and served in her until she was sunk in the Dardanelles campaign in March, 1915. Lashly was saved and after further service in the Mediterranean in the light cruiser H.M.S. *Amethyst* he was sent home.

When Commander Evans was married in 1916 the wedding sermon revived memories which had served to inspire and uplift men from all over the British Empire:

"The message which Commander Evans brought home three years ago was the first reveille which woke Englishmen to a knowledge that their ancient glory was not dead. It was the forerunner of the call to English manhood which has been so splendidly answered during the last 17 months."

Lashly was demobilized in February, 1919, and finally took up his job in Cardiff. He was 52 now, an elder statesman of pioneer days in the Antarctic. His interest never flagged. Fit and alert as ever, he was constantly in demand with his slides and magic lantern for the Antarctic lecture. He kept contact with his old friends and with none more closely than with Cherry-Garrard. He wrote to him in 1920.

> 17 Mayfield Avenue,
> Cardiff.
>
> Jan. 31st, 1920

Dear Sir,

I received Sir E. Shackleton's book *South* which you so kindly had forwarded to me from Messrs. Hatchards for which I must thank you very much indeed. I had the pleasure of hearing Wild, second in command of the expedition, give a lecture before the Natural History Society here about two months ago. He is a very good chap and did very well. Of course I knew him as he was on our "Discovery" expedition. I al-ways like to read about the travels in the Antarctic, so you may depend I shall prize it, also because it came from one who does not forget we were once plodding over the snow to try and reach our goal. I don't think we shall ever forget those times. I also like to hear other versions of the Antarctic, but I always like to see the truth as near as possible. I saw Captain Evans last Thursday. He was here giving a lecture on how we kept the seas. It was very good indeed, but of course I knew a lot about it having been at the job myself. He gave me a book he has wrote about it. He also said he was writing a book on the Antaractic. Have you seen him of late? Do you ever hear anything of Dr Atkinson? I wrote to him just before Christmas, and received a reply shortly after to say he had quite recovered his last knock out which he got in the "Glatton", except his eye, and that of course is gone for ever. He also told me he had taken unto himself a wife, but did not say who the lady was. I wonder, Sir, if you considered my letter to recommend my sister and her husband for the post you wrote to me about. I am often thinking and wondering if you have quite recovered your health, and are able to get about as in times gone by. You don't say.

> I am Sir,
> Yours faithfully,
> W. Lashly.

He went to Cambridge to see the Scott Polar Research Institute and to meet more old friends. Priestley gave him some Antarctic books to mark the occasion. Sometimes he went to Gestingthorpe Hall to stay with Mrs Oates and talk with her about her son.

In 1932 he went back to Hambledon where he built a house

which he called Minna Bluff after a familiar Antarctic landmark. He died there, soon after his wife, in 1940, at the age of 73. On his instructions, there was no headstone on his grave when he was buried in the churchyard.

Shortly before his death part of his diary was printed for private circulation. Admiral Evans wrote the foreword:

This little volume Lashly's Diary, *is a chapter from the life of one of those steel-true Englishmen whose example sets us all a-thinking.*

I owe my life to Lashly's devotion and his admirable duty-sense.

He is one of those Yeomen of England whose type gave us Drake's men and Nelson's men and Scott's and Shackleton's men, and will do so again.